My Father Harry

JOE ROBERTS

WESTBOW
PRESS®
A DIVISION OF THOMAS NELSON
& ZONDERVAN

WestBow Press books may be ordered through booksellers or by contacting:

WestBow Press
A Division of Thomas Nelson & Zondervan
1663 Liberty Drive
Bloomington, IN 47403
www.westbowpress.com
844-714-3454

ISBN: 979-8-3850-1943-4 (sc)
ISBN: 979-8-3850-1944-1 (e)

Library of Congress Control Number: 2024903496

Print information available on the last page.

WestBow Press rev. date: 05/16/2024

To: God

Dear God,

May your glory be the ink in my pen. Your gift of wisdom be the paper it is written on and knowledge the binding that holds it all together. You are the author and finisher of me and I praise your Holy name to be even lightly mentioned in your book. I celebrate this opportunity to do your will and am confident that the finished product is already finished, has been forever, and a truth that You would let me share. In Your Son, Jesus' great name I pray, amen.

Contents

Contents

Introduction

#0 INTRO:

Our Harry. How I remember Harry

Not just my father, Harry was everyone's father who knew him. He was many things to many people: neighbor, brother, father, son, husband, uncle, teacher, friend. If you were one of the many men (young and old) that worked for him on the farm, he wasn't just your boss but a partner; wanting you to succeed in whatever you chose to do. If you were one of his grandchildren, you got treated to the best hugging and "neck chewing" you could ever want. You would also have gone to the greatest bunny milk parties in the world.

When I considered all the titles I had in my head for this book, many significant thoughts came to mind as to why I even wrote it. Of course, the first reason was to show my love and respect for a wonderful earthly father. Then I wanted to point out all the many virtuous attributes that Dad had and to touch on how some of them may have come about. Another major motivator to write his story was that I saw a whole new generation coming into this world, never knowing Pap or great grandpa. Sadly, Dad passed before ever knowing anything of his great grandchildren. I pray that their parents or grandparents can pass on to them some of his wisdom. There are three verses from proverbs that come to mind. Firstly, Proverbs 23:22 NKJV: "Listen to your father who begot you and do not despise your mother when she is old." Secondly, Proverbs 1:8 NKJV: "Hear, my son, your father's instruction and do not forsake your mother's teaching." Thirdly, Proverbs 13:22 NKJV: "A good man leaves an inheritance to his children's children and the wealth of the sinner is stored up for the righteous."

Finally, I hope whoever reads this book will recognize the difference in the world of yesterday and today. For better or worse, life changes have taken place at an ever-increasing speed. Technology has exploded exponentially in the blink of an eye. I think of what my Grandmother Bertha must have thought of all the changes that took place in her life from the first airplane to space shuttles. From the roaring twenties to Rock and Roll. But nothing could have prepared her for the world we live in today. Almost everyone walks around with a cell phone which carries thousands more times the information than the first super computers had. All you have to do is ask and within seconds you will have an answer. Unfortunately, the answers are not always the truth but 'facts or opinions' of men; not buffered by any God given wisdom that the world so dearly needs. Harry was by no means perfect, but by today's standards, his wisdom brought him closer than most.

Early Memories

D o you remember the first sound you heard? I remember two. First, the call of a redwing blackbird. Whenever I've heard that sound in my life, it stirs something deep inside me. It's primal. I don't know when I heard it the first time, but I imagine that I was lying on my back and that it was Spring. Perhaps I was lying in a hamper as Mom hung clothes on the clothesline. The second sound is a beginning to an understanding of what makes up one's life. It started as an ever so slight tinkling. Each tinkling struck me as though it was solid. Like when your mother woke you up as a child; softly saying your name until you recognized who it was. This tinkling progressively grew louder and brought with it other new sounds. Sometimes like a groan, then something heavy hitting the ground. Guttural sounds that I had to see what was making them.

This was in the early 1950's. I was in a car with windows down. I knew familiar things around me like my two older brothers. Although at the time they were just familiar beings but as I struggled to position myself to find these odd noises, I realized I was with Mom. My security. I no more than felt safe, then I saw them. Huge beasts. Giants with black and white skin and wet noses. They had chains around their necks that held brass, oval shaped plates. These had individual numbers engraved on them which 'tinkled' when the excess links of chain struck them. Holstein dairy cows, pressing up closely to our car. It should have been a time for panic but as I looked at my mom to see how horrified she must be, I saw a look of joyful searching. She seemed to be looking for something very dear to her, but what? I followed her gaze past these great beasts as they continued by and felt her stir as she found what she was looking for. It was a man, bravely walking in the midst of this herd. What a figure. And as he got closer to us, I realized there was something familiar about him. Kind of like my brothers, but more. Kind of like my mom, but different. On that day I came to know two important entities of my childhood: milk cows and my father.

God has blessed me in so many ways and I can't begin to tell them all. But one of His greatest blessings to me is that I can still visit this very place where I first recognized my father. There are no buildings here, just an old dirt road with great old cotton woods shading this specific spot. These trees must be very old as to their size and I have to wonder how they have survived as I have seen so many other great trees disappear in my lifetime. The road at this place has a dip in it and a curve where my Mother pulled over for the cows. It's a place which I cannot forget and seems to be created by God just for me, so I don't forget. Over my life it is a place where special things have happened to once again bring me back to my beginning. I recall watching an eclipse of the sun right there. We were fixing fence and Dad, knowing that the eclipse was going to happen, had made a special effort to have his two welding helmets and his extra dark lenses for them so brothers Bill, Jack, and I could literally watch this phenomenon from beginning to end as very few people ever experience.

It was within one hundred yards of here that at the young age of 5, I witnessed my father use dynamite to blow up a large rock and 'hardpan' to create a crossing on a creek. I remember running with the men to a safe distance before it blew.

This is probably the best place in time to explain that this was a different time and world than what we live in now. It was a world where you grew up fast and strong. Nobody told parents what they could or couldn't do with their kids. I rode on the tailgate of a pickup truck with my brothers and other kids at the age of 6 and did it daily. Many of the things I write about may seem endangering, mean, wrong, irresponsible, or countless other failures but I will tell you for a truth, they were not. These are substances that made us the strong independent people we are today.

I will also tell you that the tales I tell of my father and my family are truthful and with God as my witness, just as it was. A different time, a different world.

Nescafé Coffee

For over fifty years, every day, seven days a week, my father would get up at 4:00 a.m. in the morning. He would go to the bathroom, silently dress, and put a teapot of water on to boil. Then he would pull out of the same old cabinet a jar of instant coffee. In all those years I can't ever remember him trying a different kind or a different method. It was always Nescafé. Sometimes I would be awakened by the whistle of that teapot, but it never whistled long. It would never reach its crescendo as he was ready to pull the pot off the stove and pour that one small cup of coffee. He would sit there in silence. The only sound now was his spoon slowly methodically stirring. He would make a slight sipping sound on this first drink but then would take his time sitting in silence, staring at nothing, drinking his coffee until it was empty. Then, just as quietly, he would be out in the darkness, gone to milk cows.

When I was old enough to remember and recognize this pattern, I thought how sad. How weird. Why would anyone put themselves through this pitiful ceremony every day? He didn't have a boss. He couldn't be fired. We lived well enough that he should be able to break from this habit if he wanted to. Why would you deny yourself the nightlife that other adults seemed to enjoy. There were times when we had 'company' visiting in the evening where Dad would just get up and go to bed. Sometimes he said good night, most times he said nothing, but once he exclaimed "I'm going to bed so you people can go home". There are two occasions in my life that keeps this mundane routine in my memory. It should easily be forgotten. But the lessons that came with these events caused me to hold dear to his way.

The second and last time happened when I was eighteen or nineteen. Dad had taught me and my brothers that if you worked like a man. Took responsibility like a man, you could make your own choices. We were also responsible for the results of those choices. He expected us to do our duties and we did our best to fulfill them. We had no curfew. We could stay out all night; but you had better be on the 'job' at the barn at 7:30.

This particular time, I came home as he was leaving. I had always timed it before coming in before he woke or, in the worst case, after he had left. This time I missed that mark. As we passed in the doorway, somewhat fearing for my life, I said "good morning!" Without stopping, he murmured "goodnight". I realized as he left that my heart was pounding; why hadn't he let me have it or at least say something critical of my lifestyle. Guilt took over my fear and I realized that the worst thing for me would be to fail him. I was at 'the barn' at 7:15.

The first-time floods me with emotion every time I recall it. I couldn't have been much more than 4 when this occurred. I woke up sick to my stomach and crying. Mom, who was always the caregiver, cleaned me up and let me lay on the couch. I know I'm not the only child who can admit this, but I couldn't throw up without my mom placing her hand on my forehead. Just a thought. This all occurred near the time for Dad to get up. As I lay there, thinking how bad things were for me, Dad came through the living room. He went into the bathroom as usual, came out dressed as usual but this time he broke the routine. He came over bent down and talked to me softly. I don't remember the conversation, but I do remember the feeling of calm that came with his attention. He went on with his normal routine but before he left, he brought me two pieces of toast with mom's homemade strawberry jam spread to the edges and said, "Maybe this will help you feel better." It did and to this day I love strawberry jam on toast especially when it has big pieces of strawberry in it. I learned that day that this hard driven man had a very soft and caring side. I learned there was more to him than just being a farmer. I learned that he cared for me.

Proverbs 14:27 NKJV

"The fear of the Lord is a fountain of life to depart from the snares of death."

I could write a book on the connection between the fear of the Lord and the fear of my father. Let me make it clear; my earthly father had lots of faults and comes nowhere close to comparing to my heavenly Father, but it is a simple truth that we are to "honor" our mother and father and you can't do that unless you fear them. I'm not talking about being scared of them. Anyone that knows the Bible understands this kind of fear. It is a perfect awe of what they can do. My pastor taught me "Fear God and fear nothing". I thank God for giving me a father that has exemplified that for me. At a very early age, I learned that if I was with my Dad, I had nothing to fear. He had me climbing 60-foot silos at the age of 4. The first time I climbed, it was between him and the ladder. When I looked down, there was nothing between me and the ground, but he continuously reassured me. "Don't look down. look up. Focus on where you are going and not where you've been. Look at where you are putting your hands and keep moving. I won't let you fall."

That was a promise and I learned real young that my Dad always kept his promises. He also never lied. If he told you that if you did something wrong again, he would paddle you, and you did, punishment was swift. Notice I said again. The first time you did something wrong, he treated it as if you didn't know any better. You might even get a short tutorial on why it was wrong. I don't believe that there was ever a third time for either me or my siblings.

There is great comfort and security in knowing that what a man or God says is the law and he does not waiver from it. It makes all their promises come true.

My father's honesty was almost embarrassing at times. He would not hesitate to tell my friends if he believed what they were doing or thinking was wrong. Oddly, he only gained their respect. Honesty is the best policy.

I can't relive any of his spankings although I know I got some. I guess that means that they were not abusive or traumatic. He would thump us once in a while. That only happened at the table or in a pew at church. These were systemic to my bad behavior (normally just being goofy or an obnoxious distraction). My Dad's hands were huge and incredibly strong. They got that way I'm sure from milking thousands of cows over the years. So, when he let that index finger fly off his massive thumb and it connected with your skull, you would immediately repent. Now if you look up the word repent, you find that it means you change directions and believe me, you would immediately be thinking differently after being corrected in this manner.

Giving you a better picture of Dad:

Harry Augustus Roberts was born in August of 1922. He was the fourth out of six children, raised on a small farm in central Ohio. There is nothing special here. Unfortunately, I don't know many details of his childhood but my love and respect for him has revealed many brush strokes that made up the man. These have come from eyewitnesses who knew and loved him as well. Some are as close as his mother and siblings. Some from almost total strangers, and many from the love of his life, my mother June.

Harry grew up in hard times. He and his family worked hard to make it, but he also came from a long line of devout Christian believers who born in him very strong moral and Christian values. There is no doubt in my mind that he 'feared' God greatly. My grandmother, Bertha, and Aunt Ruth, both told me that when he was very young his oldest sister Lucille became like a mother to him as his real mom, Bertha, was out in the fields working the farm. He often mentioned Lucille's kind and loving nature. She contracted tuberculosis in his youth and died courageously not long after she graduated from high school. One of my elementary teachers who was in her class told me of going to the bathroom with her when she was coughing up blood to help her clean up. Aunt Lucille told her she knew she was dying but it was her goal to graduate with her class. She did, but sadly was too sick to go to the graduation ceremony. Dad was fourteen Years old.

Another teacher who I had in high school, a very strict and tough old maid, treated me with abnormal grace and care. She later confessed to me that she was in the same class as my father and that he had protected her from many cruel assaults and comments from other classmates. Apparently, she wasn't favored with beauty or charm, but my Dad treated her more righteously creating in her an undying love and respect for him.

I heard from more than a couple of residents from our small town of Rushsylvania a tale of my father's strength. There was, in his high school days, a village cistern or well, in the center of town with a large and very heavy lid on it. My father was the only one who could lift it by these men's account, but Dad never told this story and only acknowledged it when old men brought the tale to light. Dad would change the subject to stories of other townspeople which gave me an insight to his past.

Dad grew up during the "Great Depression". Most of us don't have a clue to what an effect this had on the families and communities of the time. One thing I do know is that most survivors of that era are borderline hoarders. They don't throw anything away that might be used sometime. I will relate more stories on that later, but I must complete my description of this man. Why I mention the depression is because it had such an effect on my father's development as a man. There were neighbors in those days who were not farmers and therefore could not provide for their families and even though Dad's family was only existing, there was always provision for those less fortunate. It must have been a horrible yet beautiful way to learn of humility and brotherly love. Of all the stories I heard about how hard life was during this time, all were told with a great sentiment for what was gained in moral fortitude. All things are not good, but all things work for the good of those who love the Lord. My father and his family gained great respect for their charity in these times.

My father graduated from high school to the sounds of a nation being hurled into a war like no other. He immediately went into the army with all the patriotism an 18-year-old farm boy can muster. He had never been anywhere outside of Ohio at this time, but in a few short weeks, Harry was on a ship to engage in a war that would change his life forever.

Dad's stories of his service in World War Two were to me and my brothers' precious fables. It was such a rarity to have him speak of anything other than the mundane everyday life of farming. We really didn't care how a young heifer was doing after dropping her first calf or how many bales of hay had come off any certain field. We lived that. But when some other veteran coaxed him into sharing, we were spellbound. It not only put us in a part of the world that we didn't know but put us in a frame of mind of understanding how God's 'best' existed through the horrible atrocities of war. Whenever Dad shared a moment of this alien part of his life, there was always embedded a truth or reality that went straight to our young psyches, training us how real men are or aren't. He never talked about his war in the presence of anyone other than other survivors or young men like us. For myself, it placed on me a better understanding of being a protector and provider for those who need it without expecting anything in return. To be willing to sacrifice all for the good of others. I found that very sobering and still do.

War

I will attempt to paint the picture that is in my mind of Harry's War. I am sensible enough to know that after fifty years of remembering how I perceived it, it may not be how my brothers and cousins remember it. That's okay. The important thing is not the details as much as the humanity or inhumanity of it. The magnitude of this experience haunted my father until the day he died, and I thank God that I was able to recognize this as he recounted certain events over the years. The ones that I thought would cause the most trauma in his life were the ones that Dad treated most casually. It took the rest of his life to reveal what affected him the most.

Dad spoke of the trip to Europe as one of the worst experiences of his young life. The ship on which they travelled was packed to the seams with young soldiers going through a gambit of emotions. Almost all of them were embarking on an adventure of epic proportions compared to what their lives were just weeks before. Homesickness, heartbreak, anger, excitement, and fear. Mostly fear. In some respects, they had pretty good ideas of what they were getting into. Their home lives had been filled with the news of how the allies were doing. They also were well aware of sons and brothers who weren't coming home. I imagine that there were many kinds of fears for them. Not just dying, but fears like being able to be brave enough to face what was ahead. Would you be brave enough to march into gunfire? Or would you be able to kill another human? And how would you live with yourself if you did, or for that matter, didn't. I would suspect that for my father his fear was what would God think if he did kill someone. The Bible says that the fear of God is the beginning of wisdom.

By Dad's account, the emotional ride was nothing to compare to what came after they were out of sight of land and their first meal. Seasickness hit a large majority of the recruits. Those who were not sick were given the duty to clean up. It didn't take long for the rest, because of the sight smell and sounds, to join in with the vomiting. Some were sick for the whole two weeks it took to get there. Because of the crowded conditions, you were forced to share in this misery. Two weeks to get to the battle grounds meant two weeks away from home, and at least two weeks to get back to loved ones. Two weeks to anything remotely normal. It is hard to grasp, in this day and age, that you can be that far away from home. (We are only a day away from anywhere on earth now). No phones to reach across the oceans to talk to family. All correspondence travelled the same slow way as you did. Perhaps even slower due to the nature of war and how the state department could handle the mail.

I don't know many details of Dad's service I just know of the specific events that he talked about.

Dad talked of an incident of patrolling through a bombed-out city. His platoon was walking down a street, two by two, marching double file. Without warning a shot rang out and a soldier in front of Dad dropped dead. After searching for the shooter to no avail, they again reformed and continued their march. Dad just happened to look at the guy beside him at the very moment this soldier was shot in the head. I heard Dad tell this story maybe three times over a period of twenty years. The one thing that he consistently said was that this guy "dropped like a shot hog". That seems like an odd thing to say, almost cruel, but the reality of it all is that everyone who heard this knew exactly how a hog reacts to being shot between the eyes. Every time he told this it was to men who had butchered their own livestock at one time or another and this was the only way Dad knew how to explain this horrific event. I will return to this story later. There is more to it, but I want to tell the tale as it unfolded to me, over time.

He told of a soldier who acted rough and fearless. Dad said this guy was always telling stories of how brave he was in battle, a real blow hard. Then one day as they were preparing to go into action, this man breaks down and begins crying like a baby, begging them to take him home. He was shuttled back behind the lines, probably to a psychiatric ward, never to be seen again by Dad. I think Dad told this story so we might understand that the horrors of war can break the bravest of men. Other veterans would then tell similar stories that they had witnessed. Dad had a keen respect and care for shell shock victims.

The best story to me, the only one I felt I could ask Dad about, because he told it with almost joy in his voice, was when he was wounded in the Battle of the Bulge. I think he was able to speak of it this way because he experienced God's grace and mercy in letting him live. I think also that it tells of the blessings of other soldiers, medics, nurses, and doctors that kept him alive in such perilous times. Men were dying all around him, but Dad didn't.

As the story was told, Dad and another soldier were placed on point in a foxhole where they could monitor the enemy's movement and to warn the platoon if the Germans advanced. Dad was sitting on the edge of the foxhole watching for movement when a mortar shell landed and exploded in their foxhole instantly killing the other soldier and blowing my father up and out. Dad said he never heard it but that it felt like someone hit him hard in the back with a rubber boot (something we wore most of the time on the farm). When the first medics got to him, they tried to stop the profuse bleeding as much as they could as they dragged him back out of harm's way. There, with more gauze and tourniquets, they wrapped him up more, with little hope of his surviving, and put him on an ambulance that took him to a field hospital. They sewed him up the best they could and since he wasn't dead yet, they sent him on to a hospital in France.

All my life, I was intrigued with Dad's body. He had no belly button. His back had a gash in it that you could hide your hand in (which I did a few times). But the most compelling thing was that there were certain places on his shoulders and arms, where you could feel the distinct shapes of shrapnel. Because he had lost so much blood, the doctors feared he would bleed to death if they kept working on him, so they left most of the shrapnel in him and sewed him up.

Romans 8:28 NKJV tells us that "all things work together for good to those who love him." I believe that this has been proven to be true by the events in my Dad's life after this incident. Dad lay in a hospital bed for a month in France. When he finally made it home, the U.S. Army gave him a Purple Heart medal, thanked him for his service, and told him that he was 100% disabled, and that the government would pay him so much money a month for life. Six months later, Dad had to go to the VA hospital for a checkup. The doctor says "Mr. Roberts it looks like you have been getting plenty of sun. That's good, you really look healthy. And, Mr. Roberts, your hands are really rough. What have you been doing?" Dad told him "Making hay". Then the doctor said, "You can't be working; you are 100% disabled!" To which Dad retorted "Well somebody's got to do it ". The doctor replied, "but the government is paying you 100% disability!" To which Dad replied, "Well keep your money, I'm going to work". I guess that threw the department into a tizzy. It took them a few months to finally decide that if he was going to work, that they could only pay him 70% disability, which they did until he died. I remember mom telling him once "That check came today. What do you want me to do with it? To which Dad replied, "You can throw it away for all I care".

That was his character. His resolve. His connection to the government ended the day he was able to make it on his own. He never felt entitled to anything they would offer him. His service to his country was his duty as a man. He also knew that if he ever started accepting government handouts there would be conditions whereby, he would lose his freedom and self-worth. I'm not going to continue this preach now but only to say that this God given wisdom has been a fantastic gain for not only Dad but all of us kids. Later, I will tell how this resolve kept him in God's grace. Now back to his battle wounds.

Around 1964 or 65, while we were making hay one hot summer day, we came into dinner and Mom noticed that Dad's one armpit was swollen to the point of protruding. She told Dad that he couldn't work with it that way and that it was probably a boil that needed lanced and drained. You could tell by looking at him that it had to be really bothering him. He couldn't lower his arm all the way. He argued that he didn't have time to go to the emergency room and wait around on a doctor, but mom said, "Why don't you go to West Mansfield to Dr. Thompson. He will understand and get you in and out really quick." She said, "If you go right now you will be back by time to get back in the fields after dinner." I'm sure he relented more to this because common sense told him it wasn't going to get better on its own and although he didn't say it, it looked painful.

After eating, we would always take a power nap. We learned early by watching our elders that these 15-minute naps were incredibly refreshing, and we could go right back to work like new. This day Dad didn't get back in time to go to work, so Jack, Bill, and I went without him. This never happened and I assumed that Dad was going to be mad for having to wait to see a Dr. who quite frankly Dad didn't care for. Milking time came and still no Harry. I know Bill and Jack had to be wondering too, but we just went ahead and did the milking with Uncle Bud and then went home. We all went into the house to find one of our aunts there. She informed us that Dr. Thompson agreed that it was a boil and needed lanced. What it was, however, was a piece of shrapnel from that old mortar shell that had moved and pierced the main artery in his arm and what they had thought was infection was blood! I guess Dad almost bled out right there in Doctor Thompson's office. They rushed him to the hospital and got him fixed, but he had to stay there awhile since he had lost so much blood. The best part of this story is that when they removed that piece of shrapnel, a perfectly square segment of the mortar shell, there was a swastika emblem on it. Dad never bragged about his Purple Heart, but I saw him more than once show that piece of shrapnel to someone and exclaim "That ole German nearly killed me ten years after the war!"

A few days after my father passed, as we were going through some of his personal things, we came across his Purple Heart, 3 or 4 pieces of shrapnel, and something I had never seen before. Nestled with these treasures, in the back of a dresser drawer, was a stack of 30 email letters. I must explain that these emails are not the kind you see today. These emails were handwritten letters that the Army would take, read them to check their contents, then photocopy them, downsizing them to 1/4 their original size. I suppose they did this to cut down on bulk as they would be delivering tons of mail to soldiers all over the world. They were perfect miniatures of the original letters my grandmother Bertha sent to my Dad after he was wounded. As I read the first one, I became overwhelmed with emotions. What they revealed to me was what my loving grandmother was going through during this time. On the top of this stack of letters was an official notice from the United States War Department. It read:

>"Dear Mrs. Roberts,
>
>We regret to inform you that your son, Sargent Harry A. Roberts, has been mortally wounded in battle. We cannot tell you whether he is dead or alive at this time but will correspond with you as soon as we know more."

The following letters that my grandmother had written all began with little variation.

>"Dear Harry,
>
>We don't know if you are alive or how bad you are injured but I am praying to God that this letter finds you well. I know that either way you are in God's hands, and I find comfort in that."

The rest of the letters would be filled with news about his loved ones at home on the farm and friends who were also serving our great nation all over the world. Every day for a month, my grandmother wrote a letter to a son who she didn't know was dead or alive. Every day she confessed to praying to God for his life and then by faith preceded to tell Dad of his home which he must have dearly missed.

A Fearless Father

I mentioned this verse before, but it relates much more to this story. Proverbs 14:27 NKJV: "The fear of the Lord is a fountain of life to depart from the snares of death."

One quiet, warm, Sunday afternoon, (the precious time of the week that Dad could rest after the long hard hours that he worked during the week, I'm sure he lived for this two- or three-hour respite to gain some energy to face another week). Bill, Jack, and I were out in the yard where we could play and be loud and rough and not wake Dad. Suddenly, a roar came from over the hill towards Oliver's (our neighbors). We all three turned our attention that way to see a motorcycle gang pour by. Now in the late 50's, motorcycle gangs were considered the worst form of corrupt humanity. Just by their names people knew they were mean, vicious bullies who had their way wherever they went. Law enforcement would even stay clear of them for fear of the confrontation that certainly would ensue if they tried to curtail these thugs' criminal activity. The police would dutifully do their job only after several complaints and they had mustered up enough officers to do the job. Usually, the gangs would be gone before that would happen.

In total shock and awe, we watched as this gang of twenty or more bikers pulled in at the 'old brick'. The 'old brick' was a vacant brick, two story house less than a quarter of a mile from our house. My family owned it and the field on which it stood. Even though it had been empty for many years, it was still in fairly good shape. It still had all its doors and windows and a good roof. We stored things in the empty rooms. These rooms were so tight that we even used them as grain bins. We could see this group of leather wearing tough guys as they got off their "hogs". It didn't take long to realize by their boisterous voices and actions that they were drinking. I also believe they knew that the 'old brick' was empty because of its unkempt yard and the fence for cattle that went around the whole field including the house. There was a gate, but it was left open since there hadn't been any cows in there for quite a while.

My mind was racing trying to make sense of how our quiet lazy afternoon had so quickly turned into a fearful, unrealistic drama. People acting like I had never seen before. Someone in the crowd, I assume their leader, threw an empty bottle busting out a window but before it ever reached the house, brother Bill was on his way to getting Dad. I don't know if Dad was already awake from the noise, but it was only seconds before he came out of the house. Mom was right behind him trying to stop him and the terror in her voice made me weak in the knees. She pleaded that he stay here and that he couldn't go there alone. As she scooped us boys up, she said, "You're not leaving us here alone!"

In those days we didn't have a truck, just a car, probably the same one we had for my whole life

Mom no more got us in than we were off. It only took seconds to get there but the tension we all felt was palpable. In one quick move Dad ditched the old car and us on the berm of the road and was out, heading towards the transgressors. He was fearless! (at least he showed no fear). He yelled at them the same way he did at us boys when we did something terribly foolish. I don't remember his exact words, but I do know that the trespassers looked at him in disbelief. They all quickly realized that this lone man was not afraid and was willing to protect what was his with his life. The leader said something to the effect that "You ain't going to do anything about it." He got my Dad's focus, and Dad headed straight for him. I don't know what went through this guy's mind, but in a second, he shouted to his crew "let's go!!" I think he knew that if he didn't leave right then that someone was going to get hurt. If it was him, well he would lose face with the rest of the gang. But, if it was Dad, this guy would be facing some very serious charges.

I remember Dad standing there in the middle of that overgrown yard as these riders tore off around him. I was afraid one of them would hit my Dad as they left but none did, and I have to believe that they had respect for this one lone man who showed them none. Before the roar of their departure faded up the road, Dad was back in the car. He didn't say a thing, drove back home, and finished his nap.

This wasn't the only time that I saw Dad be "fearless". One Sunday evening at milking time, (our Sunday to milk as by this time in the early 70's Dad and Uncle Bud began taking turns to having a Sunday night off). Brother Jack, Dad, and I would milk on our Sunday and Bud, Chuck, and Marsha would do it on their Sunday. On this particular Sunday, Dad had gone after the cows. Jack and I got everything else ready and went out by the night-lot to help get the cows in. As usual, they came in pretty much on their own but as the last ones got closer, I heard the bull bellowing and snorting. He sounded really mad! When you grow up with these huge beasts you learn a lot about their habits and nature. This bull was a mature bull, at least 3 years old. Maybe 4. That doesn't sound old, but in bull years he is at the top of his game. I learned over the years that a bull placed in with a herd of cows becomes increasingly aggressive with time or age, and by the size of the herd. Dad and my uncles always bought good, registered bulls with good bloodlines. When they would first arrive, I always thought it was kind of funny how small and young they were. They always looked lacking compared to the old bull we had gotten rid of. In two short years, these 600-to-800-pound bullocks would turn into almost a ton of mean.

- We learned early to always watch them when you were in with them, and this was like all the time. I knew a few local farmers who had forgotten to keep one eye on the bull only to end up horribly hurt or mauled to death, their loved ones finding them when they didn't come in to supper. Uncle Bud was lucky enough to be thrown over a fence by a charging bull. I say lucky because when the bull hit him in the back, Bud went up and over the fence and not down to the ground where the bull would have ground him into the dirt like a fist into Play-Doh.

It seems to me that the 'killers' were always the docile ones. No one would expect these to attack but they would. One form of protection was to put a three- or four-foot chain on their nose ring. The idea being (and it worked) that a charging bull always lowers his head before he hits you. When he lowers his head, he steps on the chain and stops himself. This bull had never gotten a chain put on, so he was able to charge unabated. It's common knowledge that when a bull is charging and lowers his head that he can't see what's in front of him, so you step to the side, and he will run by you. Easier said than done. Most people will run and turn left or right in the process and the bull usually misses. By the time the bull realizes his target has moved you are far enough away from him to not be a target (unless you stop).

Anyway, as we waited and watched, Dad appeared first. Even at a distance I could tell he wasn't happy, and Jack made a comment that only fortified my belief. After years of growing up in abnormally tough or dangerous situations, we had acquired the ability to share our fears with humor. I really can't recall what he said but that what he said was exactly what I was thinking. Dad came towards the barn completely unaware of us and seemed to be only focused on getting the cows in and milking. Next thing that I could see was this bull's broad and muddy head as he began to crest over the hill. His eyes looked buggy almost to the point of rolling back in his head. He was extremely mad. You can't read a bull's mind but in that quick second or two, I'm sure all he wanted to do was crush this man who had separated him from his herd. He was coming hard and fast and just about the time I was going to yell,

Dad reached down and picked up an old oak 2x4 which was about four foot long, stepped to the side and swung it like a baseball bat and caught that old bull right across his snout. He had timed it perfectly. I realized that he knew where that bull was, and Dad was looking to this club to get to it before the bull got to him. Now the bull's head was down as he charged, and he couldn't see the club, but regardless Dad hit him so hard that he fell and slid on his knees. Dad kept right on walking towards the barn, and I remember making eye contact with Jack thinking that didn't just happen. Then I noticed that the bull stood back up almost wobbly and charged again! And just like the first time, right before either of us could yell, Dad turned and struck him again! He shoved dirt up with his knees and head as he slid to a stop, but this time Dad didn't keep on walking. He waited until the bull started to raise his head out of the dirt and Dad came down with that 2x4 hard on the bridge of that bull's nose not once but twice. I was sure he had killed it. It just lay there motionless. Dad came on to the barn and for the first time noticed us two boys standing there in total disbelief. He never stopped but as he passed commanded us "Don't you say a word of this to your mother". We could only nod our heads to the affirmative and neither one of us ever shared this with mom. He knew she worried about us all the time anyway and this was more than she needed to bear. He loved my mother dearly.

The bull didn't die but the very next day he took his final trip to the Kenton stockyards and I'm just guessing he ended up as dog food.

Man of Grace and Mercy and Kindness

Lessons I learned.

Bernard Pay. They say your sense of smell is your best memory. I agree. All I have to do is hear his name or remember Bernard and I can immediately smell him. That's not a fond memory but a very strong one in the fact that his odor was very strong. It was also consistent. He stunk the same every time I was near him. I won't even try to describe it except to say that it was very sour, sweaty, and old. Bernard was a prime example of poor hygiene. I would wager good money that he had never taken a bath in his adult life. I doubt that he ever owned a toothbrush or for that matter a hairbrush. He would wash his hands when he came in to eat but only because we all did.

Bernie was small in stature and although I don't know how old he was when I first became aware of his existence, he seemed old. He lived most of the time in his car which always seemed like it was on the last leg of the journey and there were never less than three dogs in it. His family of sorts. I recall a stretch of time when there were seven mutts living in that car with him. He would show up in the mornings during hay making season and would leave those dogs in the hot car all day. One day when it was particularly hot, Cousin Mike decided that these poor dogs needed to be released from this hot and putrid prison. He opened the door. One mangy little Terrier jumped out barking frantically, took off running like it was chasing something, ran in a wide circle (still barking), and never slowing down, jumped right back into that sweltering car. None of the other dogs even acted as though they wanted out even after Mike left the door open. All of us who witnessed this were astounded and still laugh about it as we recall stories about Bernie years later. There were a few stories to recall too.

Another name he went by was "digger". I assume this moniker came from his digging ditches or broken tile lines. Once after digging up a broken tile, he came in at noon to eat and as he sat at the table my mother or aunt who was there at the time, noticed a tick crawling on him. They made him go outside where they proceeded to pull several more from his exposed body. For some reason the number 27 sticks in my head. Regardless, I always wondered how many were on him in the unexposed parts. I also wondered how many he transferred to his dogs. Apparently, ticks' nest in the ground and he dug into a nest which could have thousands of ticks in it.

Bernie had a great fear of snakes. Snakes sometimes get baled up in hay bales. There were a couple of times when he refused to mow (stack) any more hay in a haymow after a snake was found dead or alive in a bale. The only time I saw him serious was when this happened. You didn't tease him about it. He would get mad. Every other time, he was happy. He was a very simple man and most of his conversations were repeating the same old jokes every day; Putting in basements for house boats and putting screen doors in submarines, followed by the same old soft chuckle "hu-hu". Now, it may seem like I am judging him but I'm not and that is the point I mean to make that we were raised to accept everyone as our equals and to treat them with the kindness that they treated us. We (being my brothers and cousins) followed the example our parents gave us. How rich a lesson in life that at the time I just experienced but now look back and realize how vital it has been for me to know how to treat others.

Mathew 22:37-39 NKJV: Jesus replied. "Love the Lord God with all your heart and soul and mind. This is the first and greatest commandment. A second is like it 'Love your neighbor as yourself.'" These are the two greatest commandments but the third is as important. John 13:34 NKJV: "A new commandment I give unto you. That you love one another; as I have loved you, that you also love one another." I must confess that I haven't always done that, but I know this is the way I should be, and my father Harry gave me great examples of how to do this. Bernard isn't the only person I will share about but what I learned through how my Dad and uncles treated him is very specific and needs its own space. I never saw him beg and I don't know anything about the financial arrangement between him and my family as to his wages, but Bernard only worked when he wanted and would just show up, my Dad always had a job for him. He was treated as a specialist of whatever that menial task might be. Even in the mow, us boys could work circles around him, but Dad gave him the unspoken duty of watching over us. My family was doing well during these years and could afford whatever we needed and more. This is the great lesson. This is how we loved Bernard; we never gave him anything he didn't ask for. My family never tried to make him more like us or improved. He never felt shame or that he had less because we never treated him that way. He was treated to anything he showed an interest in but only as we would treat ourselves. He was mysterious and wouldn't offer up much about his life or family and we didn't press. But later in his life, he mentioned to my Uncle Bud, that he would like to see his old home place in Kentucky. Bud and my Dad decided to make that happen so one early morning, us boys took up Bud's milking duties and he took Bernard home. I wish now that I would have pressed Uncle Bud to tell me more about that trip, but high school boys have other things on their minds. I know it had a profound effect on Bud. He spoke of it softly. The only real point that I do recall is that Bud took him to where his mother was buried and found out his last name was Pye not Pay.

Mr. Wilson

I don't remember his first name or much of anything else about him. I know he had a fairly large family of small kids. I know where they rented to live. An old farmhouse which was in poor repair. And even though they were always clean and neat, I know they were poor. Mr. Wilson was tall and lanky, which was pronounced by the baggy bib overalls he always wore. To hear him visit with Dad, I assumed he was pretty intelligent, and one could assume he had been industrious in the past but now, something wasn't right for the Wilsons. I don't know what caused them to be in this condition, and at nine or ten, I didn't care. Now in my sixties, I do care, and I pray to a loving God that whomever remains of the Wilson family, that all is well with them. My father, Harry, cared. I learned another valuable lesson from these two men in this one event.

One spring evening, Mr. Wilson came to the barn with a rototiller hanging out the back of his old station wagon. He proceeded to tell Dad that he had bought it somewhere cheap because it wouldn't run and that he had fixed it but needed to sell it because he needed cash. I didn't know much at my age, but I knew enough to know that this old thing was an off brand and probably a piece of junk. He told Dad that he felt it was worth $40.00 but he needed cash so if Dad was willing to take it, he would take what Dad thought it was worth. Now my young prideful heart knew Dad could buy a new one without any headaches and that he would certainly pass on this, at best, questionable garden tiller. Dad looked it over very carefully. Probably to make Mr. Wilson feel good. But then he did it. He said, " I believe this tiller, with all the work you put in it, should be worth around $150.00." I almost fell over!! Mr. Wilson said, "Now I don't have that kind of money in it and what I really need is $40.00 to get me by right now." Before he finished speaking, Harry had his billfold out and handed him $150.00. I don't remember Mr. Wilsons response. I know he offered to do anything to make it right if it didn't work. He was almost giddy as he drove off and I thought to myself 'this is where two fools met.' One for wanting to sell that piece of junk and the other one for buying it". And to think Dad could have had it for $40.00!

In all my disgust, I knew if I said what I felt, Dad would have growled at me for something I didn't understand so I just let it go. I believed that time would prove me right and then Dad would have to deal with this mess. We rolled it to the garden, beside the old hand hoe mom and Dad had always used before. He pulled one time on the starter rope, and it was running. To make a long story short; that tiller started every time with one pull. Even in the seasons to come I was always amazed that even though it had sat all winter, one pull would start it! As years passed it became my joy to be the guy responsible for being the one who worked up mom's garden, always delighting in the miracle of one pull.

There are several versus in the Bible on giving but the one that defines this lesson the best is Proverbs 28:27 NKJV: "He who gives to the poor will never want, but he who shuts his eyes will have many curses." Harry opened my eyes through this event. I thank God for giving me an earthly father who showed me through his giving kindness, that we shall reap bountifully.

The Little Man

The names have been changed to 'protect the innocent'. This story speaks of a group of people who were less than righteous, but I don't want to be judgmental. I've learned that people do what they do because they are taught to do by example. Enough said on that. On many Sunday evenings, when we were milking, we were visited in the milking parlor by a little man and his family of five kids. My short description of him: dirty and greasy. You may ask "What is a milking parlor?" A milking parlor is the room in a barn where the cows get milked. It is centered between the holding pen (where the milk cows are held before they are milked) and the milk house (the room where the milk is stored as well as cleaning supplies and other sundry items.). There is a third area where the cows go after they are milked, commonly known as the night lot.

We were one of the first dairies in our area who had a pipeline system. Once again, I feel I need to explain. When the cows came into the parlor, they would automatically be placed in stanchions. These would keep the cow in position so the farmer could thoroughly clean their udders and teats before placing the milkers on them. Rubber inflations, shaped to accept the teats, would then be placed and would stay suspended below the cow by virtue of a pulsating vacuum created by a vacuum pump (located in the pump house). This pulsating vacuum mimicked a calf sucking on the teats and would draw the milk out and up into a glass pipeline which would carry the milk into the milk house. There, the milk would fall into a large glass holding tank looking somewhat like a large water cooler bottle. When the milk reaches a certain level in the tank, another pump would kick on and pump that milk through a filter and into the main tank commonly referred to as the bulk tank. Our last tank held 1500 gallons of milk and in the best years, had to be picked up by a milk truck every two days. That tank was refrigerated and kept the milk cold at a very specific temperature. It also had an agitator in it to keep the milk stirred. Every two or three days, we would take a steel, gallon milk can and fill it for our use at home. Unpasteurized and not homogenized milk, raw milk, is the absolute best and we had all that we ever wanted anytime.

Now back to the Little Man. When he came into the milk house to visit, his kids would be all over the place and that was fine as long as they weren't bothering the cows. We even enjoyed the change in routine of socializing with people outside of our small circle. One night I walked into the milk house and was surprised to find one of the older boys filling up one of two-gallon jugs he had. I didn't know what to say or do so I walked on through as if I hadn't seen a thing. As soon as they had left, I ran into the milk house to tell my Dad. I knew he would probably get mad and take it out on this little man and tell him never to come back again. I visualized Dad beating him up! This injustice would not go unpunished I thought! Once again, I was wrong. Without even looking away from the cow he was washing, Dad said "We have enough milk." At that moment I realized that my Dad and uncle knew this was going on all along. A really good lesson I learned right then was that an offense is only an offense when you make it such. After that first time, I tried not to go into the milk house if I thought they might be in there 'stealing' milk. I didn't want them to feel bad or awkward. Also, after that time the boys in that family seemed to look at me with a genuine look of approval. It's hard to explain, but the Holy Spirit has told me that now you understand the word "Mercy."

Bob and Florida

Harry delighted In Helping others. It was if he was on the lookout for opportunities to do good.

About a mile down the road from us lived an old farmer and his wife, Bob and Florida Wagner. You might think Florida is a strange first name for a woman, but she also had a sister named California. Why their parents named them such is a mystery to me and due to how old they were then, I doubt if I could ever talk to anyone that knows. I'm pretty sure they never had children either so there is no source of learning the facts there. Bob was the only farmer I knew (outside of some Amish) that was still farming with draft horses when I was small. The horses were replaced by a small old Farmall tractor when they became too feeble to pull the plow and even though his farm was small, that old tractor and small pieces of equipment he had made the task of getting his crops planted very labor and time intensive. Bob, at best, was farming 40 acres. We were farming anywhere from 1000 to 1500 acres, using three to five large modern diesel tractors. It was the norm for us to have three five bottom plows in the field followed by two 14-foot-wide discs then a 14-foot cultipacker, which prepared the soil for planting, and finishing up before Uncle Bud came in with the planter. This sounds impressive but today two or three men with modern equipment do it in a quarter of the time.

One day as Dad took me to a field that was a couple of miles past Bob Wagner's, he noticed that Bob was struggling out in a ten-acre field on his old Farmall and 1 or 2 bottom plow. He had just finished plowing and now he would have another two to five days of work even before he could plant. Dad knew I only had another hour or so discing until I would come home to hook up to the cultipacker and then maybe three hours doing that to have the field ready for planting. He told me to pull into Bob's field on the way home and go over it with the disc for Bob. I didn't have a problem with that as I knew it would only take a half hour at the most and I enjoyed working the ground. The only problem was that Bob's gate opening was not made for this size of equipment. I was able to get in the field by being very careful and rubbing on both sides against the gate posts without doing any damage. Once I got in, I worked that small field up like it had never been worked before! I even went over it twice. I believe this soil was as loose as it had ever been, and I was sure Bob would be ecstatic. When I got to the barn, I was proud to tell how well I did. I know that Dad was filled with pride and joy; not for what I had done but with what attitude I had done it. He was probably thinking I might make a decent man some time. We hooked the cultipacker up and I was back up the road to finish our field. When I went by the Wagner's, I was proud to look at my handy work and decided when I came home, I would really finish it nicely for Bob, which I did. His field looked fantastic! I kept expecting him to come out and to lavish me with thanks. He was probably going to want to pay me something. What I had done in an hour or two would have taken him a week. I saw him at his barn. He was there, but he didn't acknowledge that I was. Maybe he couldn't hear. No, he had to know I was there.

As I gently worked that big piece of equipment through the small gate opening, I began to get some different thoughts in my head. Maybe I should take his post out with my machine or maybe I should stop and give him what for, for not being appreciative of what I had done for him. The Holy Spirit checked me though and I drove on home, still mad none the less.

By this time, Dad was milking. I put the tractor up and went into the milking parlor to share the injustice that I had received from Bob. By now, I had worked myself up as to really let Bob have it to Dad. It was time for some well-earned pity but, after I finished complaining, Dad never looked away from the cow's udder he was milking and said, "You didn't do it for you."

Luke 6:35-36 NKJV: "But love ye your enemies, and do good, and lend, hoping for nothing again, and your reward shall be great, and ye shall be the children of the Highest: for He is kind to the unthankful and evil. Be ye therefore merciful as your Father is merciful".

I don't think my Dad was much of a Bible reader and I'm pretty sure he wasn't thinking about these verses when he spoke to me, but he sure hit the nail on the head by what he said. Read those two verses again and you will understand exactly what my Dad said to me. You will also see how great a reward it is to have a father like Harry and the wisdom he shared.

Mom

How can I write a book about Harry and not have at least one chapter on mom? The truth of the matter is June, and I have to be careful how I say this, is only overshadowed by Dad because of her gender. Now I know I'm treading on thin ice for saying this, but mom is the embodiment of what God made women for. I find it very sad that people have fallen away from the perfect truth of the Bible and condemn those who cling to its teachings for the sake of equality. We are not equal! We are different! I'm not going to argue that point here because it would take away all the honor that I want to bestow upon the greatest earthly gift Dad ever got from God, my mom!

My Pastor says "A man with an argument is no match for a man with experience "so don't argue with me on this point unless you have a mother as perfect as mine.

Theresa June Morris was born on June 13th, 1927. One of ten children born to Earl and Nellie Morris. Even though they were spread out in age, these siblings were very dear to one another, and mom's very best friends were her sisters.

She was the perfect complement to Dad. Where he was hard and factual, she was soft and hopeful. No matter how tough our day was on the farm, we always came home to a warm and cheerful environment. Huge meals were always prepared for us and all we had to do was clean up and eat. I think back on it now and realize how thoughtless us boys were. We never offered to clean the table or do the dishes. We just got up and went into the living room. Mom never complained. I think she felt sorry for us because she knew how hard we worked at the 'barn'. She worked hard at keeping us boys somewhat refined and checked our hygiene daily, always making sure we were clean and presentable when we weren't farming. Hardly anyone would know this, but dairy farmer's homes have a smell very specific to them. It comes into the houses on the clothes and bodies of the people who live with the cows most of the day. It permeates anything in close proximity and if the clothes and bodies aren't cleaned soon and often, it will make your home smell like the dairy. Ours did not. Part of that might be because we lived a half mile from the barn and would get the stink blown off before we got home. Part of it was also due to the fact that Dad taught us early to wash our boots off before we left the barn. But the biggest reason was because Mom worked hard to keep things clean. When I said that hardly anyone would know this, I'm speaking as an expert on this because over the last forty-some years of working in these homes, I have become very aware of this odor. The farmers themselves don't notice it because they become used to it. It's like when you go into a smoker's home. It may almost make you sick, but they don't notice it. Mom was always cleaning. One of her favorite sayings was "cleanliness is next to Godliness". I know that's not biblical, but the Bible does say our prayers come to God as an aroma which he smells. Another saying was "make sure you have clean underwear on. What if you're in an accident?"

Mom, like Dad, was raised during the depression. She was very frugal with us kids but did it in such a way that people thought we were much wealthier than we were. One of my favorite stories to tell of this speaks volumes of her skill.

Mom bought an old wool suit for Bill when he was around eight or nine years old. She paid fifty cents for it. Brother Bill wore it every Sunday to church until he had outgrown it. Brother Jack by that time could wear it and did so, every Sunday, until he grew out of it. By that time, I had grown enough that it fit me and like Bill and Jack before me, I wore it every Sunday until I couldn't wear it anymore. You would figure that by that time that old suit would have been destroyed by us three boys, well not so. It was still nice enough to give it to my cousin Chuck and later was given to Cousin Me. There were no more boys after Mel to hand it down to and I have wondered what the final end to that fifty-cent suit was. What a time to be alive! A time when people were reverent to church and wore only their Sunday best there. The only other time you wore those clothes were to weddings or funerals. Mom taught us respect for those occasions by how she treated those clothes. I'm sure she spent a whole lot more than fifty cents on dry cleaning that old suit over the years and kept all our 'good' clothes in good repair and clean. She taught us how to polish our shoes and I delighted in buffing them to a shine. She instilled in us such a sense of worth in how we presented ourselves that we wouldn't dare play in those clothes but usually couldn't wait to get home to throw on some rough clothes.

Her ability to graciously take one boy's clothes and hand them down to the next was so uncanny that even when we were in high school and could afford our own clothes, we still would wear each other's as if they were our new clothes.

In my early years, Mom raised chickens. I don't remember too many egg layers but mostly meat chickens. She would buy fifty to one hundred at a time as day old chicks. We would pick them up in the car and I'll never forget the sound of all those chicks peeping as mom drove home. They would be in cardboard boxes with heavy cardboard lids on them and holes perforated all around the box for air for them. These holes were just big enough to stick your finger in to get pecked or to see a tiny beak stick out occasionally. They also let out the aroma of these baby chicks and for a truth, they never stunk, but had a smell that once you've smelled it, you never forget it.

It doesn't take long for these chicks to become full grown fryers. Mom could and would occasionally kill and clean them herself. It was the only job I knew she detested. It wasn't the butchering part but the killing she hated. Her method was to gently place the birds head under a piece of wood lathe (a one inch by quarter inch by sixteen-inch strip of wood) on top of a small slab of cement. She would step on the two ends of the lathe and holding the hen by its legs would give a quick jerk, pulling its head off. She would nearly fling the headless chicken away from herself probably to escape the flying blood, but I think mostly out of disgust of what she had just done. The term "running around like a chicken with its head cut off "takes on special meaning for a young boy who experienced this a few times. I remember the horror of being chased up the cellar steps by one of these headless, flopping monsters to only return to the same spot to experience the thrill again!

I find that as I write about mom, what I know and love about her can't be written in a chapter. She is a book unto herself. I will endeavor to just hit some highlights about her.

She made our home. It was always the place I wanted to return to. There was always comfort there, always love.

She taught us how to dream of finer things. I remember sitting on the couch with her looking through catalogs picking out bedspreads and curtains for our rooms, her engaging us to tell her what we liked. What makes this a big deal to me is that just an hour or two earlier, us boys were up to our necks in cow manure and work, with very little spirit or joy in life. Now we were washed and fed and warm and given hope of better things to come. Almost every night she would gently rub our backs; her long graceful fingers miraculously pulling the tension from our bodies. Sleep came easy. Even today, at ninety years of age, from her oldest son to her youngest great grandchild, her back rubs are a wonderful gift.

I could go on and on about mom but will save that for a book about her.

The last and maybe the most important thing I'll say about her is that she loved my Dad Harry, deeply. They never fought, at least in front of us kids and always enjoyed each other's company. In the fifty some years that they were married, and Dad would be coming in from the barn, she always was glad he was home. Once again, I thank God for such a loving mother and pray that all children should be so blessed.

The Hoarder

I mentioned that my father and mother grew up during the "Depression". Most people in my age group, if they were paying attention, would have learned some peculiar things about our elders during this time. The effects of the depression were so great that it caused this generation to do things that we would think irrational. One of the most obvious was that they became hoarders. The common thread which I learned from these dear elders was everything has a value if you can't afford better. They were never going to be caught again needing the most menial items. To prove my point, look in your great grandparents' cabinets. How many old, whipped cream containers do you need? Or pieces of aluminum foil or string. It may seem silly to us but if you look deeper into their thinking, much more is revealed. That whipped cream container or butter bowl makes a good cereal or soup bowl. Much better than the tin cans they may have had to use. These bowls also make great storage containers for anything from leftovers to buttons. I found that they took great pride in innovating new uses for the junk they had. They also felt a responsibility to have these things available to others less fortunate than themselves.

The Bible tells us to honor our mother and father. Self-centered people think that doing this is for the old people's sake. But the reality is that by doing this, we get blessed. We gain wisdom that you can't get from books. We get an insight into the basest fundamentals of the human condition. We learn humility.

I thank God for the opportunity to have learned how this era in history affected my loved one's lives. I pray that we never have to go through a similar thing but if we do I believe we would in the end be the better for it.

I also believe that the effects would be much, much more devastating to this generation which has become so dependent on all their needs being met by money and if something doesn't work out right. Throw it away and get new.

Let me digress. My Dad took great joy in hoarding. He wasn't messy about it, in fact, half his joy came from being organized in it. He was a great welder, fabricator, and mechanic. He loved working in his shop on things, mostly farm equipment, but anything would do. If it could be made or fixed, Harry could do it. He kept every little piece of iron or steel he could find. You never know when that 3-inch piece of angle iron will be the perfect brace for something else. He remembered these bits and pieces too. When he would come to a point where he needed a particular scrap item that he had ferreted away somewhere, he would spend the time to find it.

I loved being in the shop with him. He was poetry in motion there. As I grew older, he would ask me to get him something specific from a specific pile of scrap. At first, I hated this. It seemed impossible to find what he was asking for and I would give up looking and whine about it not being there. He wouldn't say much but when he would go to where I was supposed to be looking and pick up the piece he asked me to get. He had a way of looking at me that made me feel three inches tall, but like our Heavenly Father, he never gave up on me, and over time, I delighted in searching out the prize. I also learned the method of his madness and began to bring him stuff I thought he could use.

Once, a neighbor, John Jacobs, called Dad and asked if he could use his pickup truck. John's father had died, and John needed to clean his father's basement out so they could sell the house. In those days, most every farmer had a ditch or ravine where they hauled their trash. The benefit of this was that it helped control erosion. It worked well and most farmers let the neighbors use their dumps if they wanted to. John wanted to haul this junk back to our dump as well as use the truck. Dad told John, "I'll do you one better. I'll send Joe up with the truck Saturday morning and he can help you load it and haul it out here himself." Well, John really appreciated this, and I was happy to get off the farm for half a day, drive the pickup to town, and to explore a city house. Everything went well. John's father and John himself were very organized so everything to go to the dump was in cardboard boxes that were easy to load and handle. It wasn't long until I was pulling into the driveway to our farm. Now our farm was back a long lane and as soon as I turned in, I saw my Dad watching for me to come. At 17 years old I had learned my father's habits well enough that I knew he wasn't going to just let me drive by to the dump. No, he was going to have to rummage through this junk to see if he could find anything of value. Sure enough, he stops me and asks, "So what all you got in there?" My reply was, "Look Dad, it's just a bunch of junk from an old dead man. Let me take it back and throw it in the dump." But that didn't deter Dad. He said, "Old man Jacobs took good care of his things. I'm sure there is some good stuff in here." The whole time he was talking he was looking. I begged "Please Dad, just let me take it to the dump." I no more said that than he reached in the back and pulled out an old pair of

Redwing work boots. I was not enjoying this one bit. "There's a lot of good wear left in these shoes. " He said to which I replied, "Dad! They're just an old pair of a dead man's shoes! Let me take them to the dump." He was undaunted. "I believe these shoes would fit somebody." (Oh no, I thought.) "I believe these shoes would fit you." he said.

I don't think I had ever been so mortified. How could he expect me, one of the coolest kids in my school, to wear these old shoes. One thing I knew, when he told me to try them on, the arguing was over, and I better try them on! I felt a little bit like the reverse Cinderella. I was praying and expecting these junk shoes not to fit, and I could haul them back to the dump which would be their most appropriate grave. But no, they fit like gloves. So much so that I really didn't want to take them off. But then reality set back in, and I needed to get them off and figure out a way to not be caught wearing them. My pride was unbearable in those days, and I think this was Dad or God's way of having me deal with it. That next Monday morning I put those old shoes on, went to school expecting to be the laughingstock of the day, only to find that no one cared or noticed, and I ended up wearing those beautiful old Redwings for ten years after I was married. I doubt that I'll ever own a better pair of shoes.

The Horse Pull

This story doesn't tell of my father as much as the time. There are many traces of Dad in this story but again it is mostly about how things were in 1960.

2nd Corinthians 6:14 NKJV: "Be ye not unequally yoked with unbelievers." Mathew 11:29-30 NKJV: "Take my yoke upon you and learn of me for I am meek and lowly of heart: and ye shall find rest unto your souls. For my yoke is easy and my burden is light."

There was a man up the road who had never been married and by most people's standards, poor. For a six-year-old boy, he was somewhat of a mystery. He would just show up at odd times either at the barn or our house. My greatest attraction to him was that he owned a great buckskin horse whose name I have forgotten but the horse was magnificent and very gentle. He was the first horse I ever got to ride. I will never forget the smell of that great steed or the saddle that Sam put on him. Sam's real name was Corwin, but I knew him as Sam. He always treated me with the respect of an older person which I loved, and I became jealous when I found out that he treated all kids that way. Even though he never married or had kids of his own, he basically adopted everyone he met. This is the first big contrast between now and then. Today this kind of relationship with children would be scrutinized. Another thing I remember about Sam is that every Christmas he would stop at our house and give Dad and mom a bottle of Morgan David wine. Now my parents were not drinkers. We never had any alcohol in our house except that one yearly bottle of Morgan David wine. My brothers and I would coax our parents into letting us taste it every year and we really thought we were getting away with something. The rest of the year that bottle would just sit there until the next year and the new one arrived.

I believed Sam was a real cowboy, at least he was the closest thing to one that I ever met. He had a chunk of property (probably 5 acres) which had outhouses, a corral, and maybe some bleachers for people to watch him and several other horse people ride. They were a club called "The Rushcreek Roughriders." Years later they moved from his property to a new more modern facility outside of Rushsylvania. It's still there.

One cold fall night Sam showed up at our place and asked if anyone wanted to go to a horse pull up in Kenton at the Hardin County fairgrounds. Of course, brother Bill, age 10, Jack, age 8 and I, 6 years old wanted to go. I vaguely remember my mom having some concerns about us going but when Sam pulled in our drive, we were out the door. Parents wouldn't let this happen today. Sam's old car wasn't in really good shape. We had to hold the right rear door shut, which also had no glass in the window. I don't believe I ever felt so cold after that 20-mile ride in freezing weather, with my arm holding the door closed. On the way home Jack got the job. Once there at the fair arena, I recall Sam getting out and heading in without ever looking back to see if us boys were keeping up. It was pitch dark out as we entered the building. Then as I hurried to keep up with Jack and Bill, I found myself standing right between two huge draft horses. I had been to pony pulls before and had watched them from the stands. I had been impressed by their power and drive, but ponies are ponies and aren't necessarily that big, but this was a horse pull and these draft horses were gigantic!! I have often wondered how I could have gotten myself in this place so many years ago and come out of it unhurt. It is one of those rare moments in time that I believe God puts us into to show us something wonderful, beautiful, and incredible that affects how we deal with the issues of life. When I realized where I was, how close I was to these beasts that I could run under without hardly bending over, I forgot about where my brothers or Sam were. This was every man for himself, and I needed to find a way to safety fast. I'm standing inches away from the knees of these marching and stomping giants. As I spin around to retreat, I'm looking straight up at an oncoming nose that is bigger than my head. I am surely going to be trampled into the sweet-smelling sawdust and horse manure in which I'm standing but by the time I could take my next breath, this horse and his team partner gently veered off their course leaving me standing there in total awe. The sounds were incredible. Chains clinking and rattling, horses snorting and whinnying.

And then the drivers; old potbellied men leaning way back on their lead lines, or reigns, that they had hooked over their shoulders. Each one shouting or barking out orders to their teams "Haw Jim, Haw Jess." "Git on Ben." Somehow, I had survived. Now I take in the rest of my surroundings. Above the horses' heads (which are probably seven or eight feet up) there is a cloud of smoke which only gets thicker as I look farther. Almost every man here is smoking a pipe or cigar, mostly cigars. The number of men whose cheeks are sticking out with a chaw of tobacco, like they have a baseball in there, makes up the difference. You mix that smell with the horses, and you smell an aroma that will seldom be repeated today. I thank God for the opportunity to have experienced it.

By the time I found my brothers, Sam was already sitting almost at the top of the stands. This was one of those rare occasions where brother Jack showed some concern for my welfare. I remember him telling me to "come on" as we made our way up to Bill and Sam.

Here is where the real meat of this story comes into play. I accidentally found out recently that most people don't know what a horse or pony pull is. This really dates me, and after getting over the sad fact that I'm an older man, I realize how privileged I am to have experienced these events.

How a pull works. There is a sled of sorts, with a steel framed cage in which cement blocks are stacked to give it weight. The object is to see what team of two horses, or ponies, can pull the most weight the farthest. You want your team to make a full pull to go to the next round. A full pull is when a team pulls that sled the entire length of the course. I don't remember the length, but I'm thinking it is 25 ft. After each round, they add more blocks. Today, I believe you couldn't have pulls because PETA or some other animal rights activists would proclaim this as cruelty to animals, but I will tell you a truth; these animals were bred and raised to pull, and you could sense how much they loved it. These aren't just horses but well-trained athletes. Pulling horses don't have bits in their mouths but the term 'chomping at the bit' fits in really well right here. They can't wait to pull!

There is a driver and a hook-up man. It's a scary job hooking up a team. They are constantly wanting to lurch forward before they are hooked up. They only want to go forward. A driver could get them to back up a few feet but if they heard the hook clinking onto the chain of the sled attached to the whippletree of their harness, they would immediately lurch forward into the pull. If the man hooking them up didn't make the connection on the first try, the driver would have to bring them around again for the hook up.

Once that connection is made, the hooking man only had a second to get out of the way of the sled.

Now the key to a good pulling team is that both horses have to be equally matched in strength and size. They must also hit the resistance of the tug at the same time. This is what it means to be equally yoked. One horse alone can't budge the load but two working in unison can get it started to move. I believe pulling horses love this task. When they lean into the harness with all their strength, they will sometimes go clear down on their knees, muscles bulging, nostrils flaring, and their eyes looking as if they have seen a ghost. All the weight is on the neck collars, which ride on their shoulders. If one slips or goes down the other horse has the whole load. If he can't keep it moving, he will stop to try to jerk it started again but usually the team is out of sync by this point and the pull is done. Both horses will keep trying until the driver commands them to stop. They will be unhitched and will prance out of the arena as the next team comes in.

It states in 2nd Corinthians 6:14 NKJV: "We are commanded to be ye not unequally yoked with unbelievers." We as Christians can't do what God wants us to do if we only associate with unbelievers. We need to be equally yoked with people of the same convictions as ourselves to get the task done. Whatever it is that God commands us to do, we need other team members to help us make this 'pull' and there is no better one to be yoked with than Jesus Christ our lord. He tells us in Mathew 11:29-30 NKJV: "That if we will take his yoke on us, if we allow Him, He will do the work for us and make our burdens light." That doesn't sound like you are equally yoked, but he says, "to learn of him that he is meek and lowly of heart". What a wonderful savior who is willing to carry our burdens for us. To come down to our low level of being to lift us up and give our souls rest.

Killing Rats

In the 60's we, young men, youth, were tasked with much more credit of responsibility. If you want to make a society irresponsible, take away their natural God given sense to be responsible. Tell them they can't take care of their own business and watch as they sit back and watch others take over. The sad part is we lose freedoms that compel us to be better. We lose the ability to make sound decisions and take bold risks. We become spineless, and worst of all fearful. Fear is to Satan, as faith is to God. God hates fear and tells us that the only thing to fear is Him!

That's a long way around to begin this story but is important to show the different mindset people had then. There is so much more to say about what we have freely given up as men, but this is not the place for me to chase that rabbit. Hopefully this tale will reveal some of what we have lost or given up.

Every fall our schools FFA would put on a pest hunt. For those of you who don't know, FFA stands for Future Farmers of America. It was the best training you could get if you weren't going to college to be a professional at something (even though there is no greater profession than farming). I always assumed that other schools put on pest hunts as well, but I don't know that for a fact. The idea behind it was to see who could kill the most pests on the farm. I won't assume that everyone reading this knows what pests are, so I'll give a little rundown on them. Any animal (non-domesticated) that causes loss of product or carries diseases falls into this category. Each species was given a point value as to how much damage they could do or the harder they might be to get. Sparrows: those sweet little songbirds that are so common on the farm were worth 2 points, proven by bringing their heads to school. Mice were the same. Rats moved up the scale to 10 or 25 points. I don't remember. Crows were 50 points, raccoons 100, and foxes were 500!!

Pidgeon's were, if I recall right, 20 pts. All these creatures could cause a lot of damage on a farm if left unchecked and all good farmers had ways to reduce their numbers. Oh! I just remembered groundhogs. I don't remember how many points they were worth, but I believe it couldn't have been enough as I tore the whole front end off of a tractor by accidentally driving into one of their boroughs. We will talk about that later.

A common sight to see at school during that week or two of the pest hunts were high school boys with their car trunks open. This allowed anyone who was interested to see how well they were doing. It also allowed us a chance to check out what type of guns they had. The teachers (men) were just as guilty at bringing in their weapons as well. From the first grade to the twelfth, us hunters hung around as long as recess would allow. I might add, no one ever got shot. This also brings out another point of being responsible; even though there were many levels of killing power, everyone always opted for the safest method for the situation they were in. For a crow flying high outside, you needed a good shotgun but for a mouse or a sparrow roosting in the rafters of a barn, nothing bigger than a BB gun would be used. You wouldn't want to put holes in the metal roof, and you didn't want ricochets. My brothers and I found that if you flushed a sparrow out of a rafter (usually by throwing grain at them) they would fly directly towards the spotlight shining on them allowing another guy to 'swat' or 'bat' the bird out of the air. It didn't take too long to clear our grain sheds of perching sparrows or pigeons.

Rats were another story. It was reported in an Ohio Farmer magazine once that for every rat you saw on your farm, there were a hundred you didn't see. I believe that this was a true statement because of several instances where after trying to ferret out the one rat I saw, I would get into large nests of several rats.

Our neighbor's farm was really infested with rats. You would see two or three of them scampering into hiding whenever you came into sheds that weren't frequented a lot by people. It might be because the lady of the place raised dogs. Show dogs, and rats seem to love dog food.

The neighbors also had a son who fell in age right between Jack and Bill. That put Randy three years older than me. Randy is a book in himself. I learned many things from Randy and almost everything he taught me was not good. I suppose that is why both my brothers and I liked to "hang out" with him. It is also why they never wanted me, the little brother, to be a part of their adventures and why I wanted to all the more. I found out that if I begged mom to let me go with Bill or Jack when they had plans to go to Randy's, she usually made them take me along. She probably thought that my presence with them would curb their mischief but all it did was make them threaten me more on what they would do to me if I told of any of the wild things they might do. The more they tried to force me to go home and leave them to their frivolity, the more I would try to prove myself as being as cool as they were.

One cool and dark night, during a pest hunt, I forced Jack into taking me along to Randy's. their goal was to see how many points they could get by killing rats. I thought it was odd how easy it was to persuade Jack into taking me until we got there and heard Randy tell me what they expected me to do. Of course, if I didn't do my job, I could forget about ever doing anything else with them again. They even upped the ante by saying I would be branded as a coward if I didn't perform this menial task. Randy explained all I had to do was crawl under the corn crib and make my way through all the junk that had been shoved under there for several years and come out the other end. This doesn't sound too bad except this corridor of tetanus cutting rusty metal is fifty foot long and there is no easy escape; you have to go to one end or the other to get out. The floor of the crib was only 18 to 24 inches above my head and the width between the concrete footers was 4 feet. Being urged to make a quick decision, I reasoned that any rat I might confront would flee in front of me away from my flashlight light. I also envisioned the praise and respect I would get when I would come out the other end. I would be in with these guys forever I could hear them telling the tale as they showed the whole school their pile of rats. Abruptly I said, "I'll do it!" Hand me that flashlight". "We can't give you the flashlight" Randy said. "We need it to see the rats to kill em". Now that's just ignorant. No one would crawl through there at night without a flashlight! "How am I supposed to see where I'm going" I asked. Jack, who always seemed to make sense told me "Just crawl towards the light. We'll keep your way lit from the other end. Besides you will have a hard time getting through if you have to hold a flashlight". I had to admit to myself that he made a good point and as I thought about all the fame and glory, I was sure to receive, I began.

The light at the end of the tunnel seemed so distant. It didn't illuminate my path at all, but it gave me something to focus on, a goal of sorts. I decided if I took my time, made sure my hands and knees were not placed on anything sharp or unstable, moved slowly and deliberately that I would make it through. Much of the junk in front of me was silhouetted in the light. This gave me markers to work to and around. Occasionally the light would flicker and be gone leaving me in total terror. Apparently the two "killers" felt like they needed to survey their surroundings. A quick yelp from me would put them back on point. Halfway through, I was filled with a mixture of fear and exhilaration. Fear because I knew I was the farthest away from escape as I could get. When I looked back to see where I had come from it sent chills down my spine. I don't think I had ever seen such a foreboding space. Looking forward, I realized that I was just a few yards away from being anointed "BRAVE."

Every once in a while, I could hear those guys whispering and giggling. I'm sure in disbelief that I had done this bold act. It was at about this time that I started noticing other activities. First was the sound of something light going across a piece of sheet tin roofing

I was crawling across then looking to the light through all the silhouetted objects, I saw movement. Not much, something small but movement then two then more. By the time I realized that what I was seeing were rat bodies, the first one hit me in its mad retreat to the darkness. Jack and Randy Began whooping and hollering and I was praying that they were killing all the ones that hadn't run over my back!

I stopped worrying where my hands and knees were hitting. I cleared the last ten feet in record fashion. I thought for a split second; what if they clubbed me as I come out? I didn't care. I shot out from under that corn crib like a ball out of a cannon. I even think I might have scared Jack and Randy some.

I remember lying on my back on that cold, damp ground and as I gained my composure, I tried to put on the face of someone who wasn't afraid to put himself through this type of calamity at any time. And as I sat up to gaze on the pile of rats that I knew these two had to have killed, the same mess of rats that would prove my heroics the next day at school, I realized that these two jay birds hadn't killed the first one. After I spent a good minute yelling at them and telling them how worthless I thought they both were, they laughingly admitted that every rat that came out ran right back in to me before they could react.

I didn't gain any recognition for my bravery the next day at school and maybe Randy still saw me as Jack's punk brother and even though I don't remember us ever talking about it after that night, I will always believe that me and Jack took one step closer to being friends and not just brothers.

Learning Responsibility

The fair

Harry had occasion to teach us responsibility wherever it could be taught. Looking back, I realize that most of the time, I didn't want to be taught. I would rather mom or Dad be responsible. We live in a world where a liberal society shuns responsibility and expects the government to take care of us. It has gotten so bad that this lazy society asks that we all just be equal. Even though you may have been very diligent in your work, you need to give it to that sluggard who has never done anything for himself even though he could. Today these irresponsible people want all sports to not be competitive. If one child has aspired to be great at something and has worked hard to get better, to be the best, this corrupt world says that makes the lazy child who doesn't even want to perform feel bad so let's not have winners and losers.

If you look up responsibility in the Bible, you will find several verses which instruct us. But the one that I feel explains this the best is Galatians 6:7NKJV: "Do not be deceived, God is not mocked; for whatever a man sows, that he will also reap." Another one is Proverbs 22:6NKJV: "Train up a child in the way he should go, and when he is old he will not depart from it". Dad trained us early and often to be responsible for what we owned and what we did or said.

Every summer, right between the second cutting and third, when we had just finished wheat and oats and making straw, when we had worked our hardest, came the county fair. For most kids this was a time when you would spend a day or maybe two there, riding rides, meeting other kids from around the county and seeing a little bit of farm life in the form of show animals.

For us, this was our vacation. We loaded up our show calves and cows along with hay and feed and straw and our show trunks or boxes and would head to Bellefontaine to the Logan County Fair. I loved the show boxes. To me, they were like treasure chests. When you opened them up, the aromas that drifted up out of them were toxic. The first thing you noticed was the smell of leather. The smell of well-polished or oiled halters that were only used one or two times a year to show your heifer. They weren't cheap and we treated them better than we did our own dress shoes. Then came the scent of soap from large bars that we washed our cows with. There was talcum or baby powder that we put on their tails to make them fluffy and white and shoe polish for their hooves. On top of all that, the smell of rope from the extra halters that we used every day. We also used the box to put all our other treasures in too. Show boxes made great seats also. You could sit on them all day and watch people pass through the dairy barn.

The fair would consume us kids for a week. We got out of all our regular farm chores to focus on the fair. At the age of nine, I got in the stock truck with all my cousins, went to the fairgrounds, and didn't return until the end of the week. That meant living there twenty-four hours a day for six days. The only time I would see mom was when she would bring me clean clothes every day. Mom would come on show days as well to watch us show. She and Dad also always came on Sunday so we all could eat as a family. I did this until my junior year.

Here is where the responsibility comes in. We had to make sure our livestock were taken care of. We had to make sure they were clean. We had to make sure we were registered for our classes, our paperwork was done, and most importantly, we were ready to show when it was showtime that meant washing and prepping the cow and getting yourself cleaned and dressed in your show clothes. This consisted of white pants and shirt. In the seven years that I was in 4-H and showed at the fair, I only owned one cow. I bought her with my own thirty dollars from my Dad and uncles. She was born on Christmas morning, so I named her Christy. There in that warm barn on that cold Christmas morning, I believe I was filled with more affection for that calf and hope for the future fair than I have ever felt and although Christy never took first place, I never gave up on her. She was a good milking cow. I didn't get paid for what she produced. I always thought that the milk was pay for Dad feeding and keeping her. I only had a set amount of money for the fair, so I became responsible with it to get me through the week. Once it was gone, it was gone.

Before I leave the fair, I feel compelled to tell another truth about it. Our dairy, Roberts Brothers Farms, was one of the largest if not the largest dairies in the county. In all the years that we showed cattle, thirteen kids, we never won first place. We always got blue ribbons but no firsts. My Dad and his brothers were never on the fair board, yet the smallest dairy farmers were and their kids' cows always won. The point I need to make here is not that we were treated unjustly but that we never complained and always had hope for the next year. My Dad never complained so we never complained. That's a whole new level of being responsible!

My junior year I got my license to drive and even though I had been driving for a few years, now I was legal. I bought what I could afford, and it was a beautiful red and chrome Honda 350 motorcycle. I didn't own a car until after I graduated because I didn't have the money. If I needed to go anywhere in the cold or rainy weather I could either borrow mom's car or Dad's truck or if I was really lucky, Jack or Bill's car. I was also not against riding with any of my friends who owned cars. I did that a lot. But if it was warm enough to ride, I rode. My motorcycle was very unique. Not really by anything I had done but brother Jack. He had bought it originally brand new from the dealer. It was a 350 scrambler which meant its design was for on or off-road riding and those 350's had more chrome than color. He immediately took the gas tank and seat off and put custom ones on then he took the handlebars off and put high ones or "ape hangers" on it. His goal I'm sure was to make it like a chopper but soon realized no matter how much he did to it; he would still end up with a Honda. In the process he created a bike which not only I loved, but all my friends loved as well. They were envious. Many tried to duplicate it in one form or another but mine was the best! Again, not by anything I had done, but Jack. The funny part of this is that it was like two fools meeting. I'm sure Jack was ecstatic to find someone foolish enough to give him $750.00 (the original store price) for a perfectly good Honda that he had torn apart. I, however, couldn't believe he was naïve enough to sell it for a loss after all the work he had put into making it so special. He immediately went out and bought an old Harley Davidson and built the chopper that he wanted while I enjoyed every moment I could being on my bike exploring the world

That summer, instead of going to the fair, I worked harder but took a week with a friend and rode our bikes to Kentucky. As I mentioned before, if you worked like a man then Dad felt you deserved to play like a man and as all the main work was done for a week or two, he allowed me to go. There was no set time to be back, no set destination, and no communication for the duration. This was before cell phones and I guess, mom and Dad thought no news was good news. A week or so before we left, all the local boys were jeering us and taking bets on how far we would get on such small machines. A 350 Honda is bad enough, but my friend had a 250 Yamaha. It was questionable. To make this long story shorter, we made it to our destination in southern Kentucky and we're living large for four or five days. I had no designs on coming home right away but the Holy Spirit prompted me to head home. I think he must have moved on my friend John's heart as well because when I mentioned leaving, he agreed. We got home on the last day of the fair. Mom met me with a look of relief, but I sensed some sadness. My grampa Fred had died the day after we left and had I not come home, I would have missed his funeral.

As I look back on that event so many years ago, I realize that my heavenly Father had other reasons for me being there than just being with family. That was reason enough, but He showed me what peace there is in death if you believe in Him. The Roberts family celebrated grampa's life and death. We saw that his troubles were over, and he was finally going home. Grampa Fred had been diagnosed with "hardening of the arteries". I think that is what we know as Alzheimer's. For several months, he would run away from his home and the whole family would have to search for him. When he was found and asked, "Where are you going?" He would always say, "I'm going home. I have horses to feed". He hadn't owned a horse for years, but in his mind, he was that young man who had horses but no wife or kids. Usually, when he ran away, it was up county road 5. He had to walk past one of his three sons' houses so he could be found or seen easily enough. Sometimes, when Gramma Bertha was still alive, she would call and send out the alarm "That ole fool has took off again." There are many funny yet sad stories about him during this time but too many to write about now. The absolute most incredible part of this chapter needs to be told now.

When and where do we learn responsibility? I think the best answer to that is by watching the examples set before us. Responsible people have responsible parents and children. This follows God's teaching, if a man is righteous then I will bless his household for three generations. I know that's not how the Bible says it but that's how the Holy Spirit reveals it to me. I don't want to get into a lot of theological verbiage so instead here is the example.

My wonderful grandmother Bertha Ansley Roberts, who lived through many hardships and worked hard all her life, had a disease called dropsy. What is characteristic of this disease is that your legs and feet retain water and swell to the point where for all the years I knew Gramma, she couldn't wear normal shoes. What she wore was somewhat like sneakers but the tongue and top of the shoe would be cut out. Her legs were like tree trunks, just straight with no definition, no knees. If they got bumped or scratched, they would seep for days. She never complained and kept cooking and housekeeping with thirteen grandkids running in and out of her house. She gradually went from walking with a cane to a walker then to a wheelchair until she finally became totally bedridden. She always felt so bad that she had to be lifted by a special hoist to be cleaned or go to the bathroom. Meanwhile, Grampa Fred was deteriorating to his disease (Alzheimer's). It soon became imperative that they both needed twenty-four-hour care. To my knowledge, it was never discussed about putting them into a nursing home. Instead, each of the four couples took turns being with them. On the days that mom and Dad watched them, I occasionally took the time to sit with them and was blessed by many stories from Gramma. To this day, one of the best compliments I ever got was when she told me how much I reminded her of her father. How she described him with such fondness made me feel very special. She died first. I often thank God for that because Grampa at that time didn't recognize her as his wife. She was just some lady there in that bed. Now you would think that this would be the time to put him in a home, but my family saw him as their responsibility, and you took care of your own even if he didn't know them. Once in a while he would know where he was at and was in his right mind, but it became less and less often and for shorter periods of time. I was sitting with him one evening while he was sleeping, and mom and Dad were doing things around his house. He woke up and looked over to where Gramma had lain and then to where she always sat. She had died before this time, so she wasn't there. He looked at me and said, "Mom died hasn't she." I told him yes. It wasn't two weeks later that he passed. I remember the preacher, Al Holzboaur, stated that he had never seen a more joyful funeral. He said, "That's the way it should always be if you know that they are going to paradise." Grampa had been a funny and creative man for us all but most importantly, he believed in God.

One final story on responsibility. That next summer (before my senior year) my friend John and I planned another cycle trip. For a year we had mesmerized our friends with stories of our first trip. Now, they wanted to do it over with us. We were like the leaders of this pathetic cycle gang and pride had us wanting to show them how it was done. The trip was planned, and I worked diligently to get my work done so this could happen for me. I worried and fretted for a month thinking something would go wrong and we wouldn't be done making hay on the day we were to leave. In my haste to see it get done, I became careless and walked right in front of one of our biggest tractors. Cousin Chuck was driving and paying attention to where the hay wagon was positioned to the elevator. He didn't see me as that was not his job. He was doing exactly what he was supposed to do. The front tire of the tractor caught me at the knee and pushed me over sideways. In an instant it was driving up my legs towards my knees. I screamed and thank God Chuck heard me. He reacted quickly and stopped the tractor with the wheel sitting on my legs just below the knees. He had a look of horror on his face as I yelled for him to back off. He shifted the transmissions into reverse and backed off my legs. I pulled myself out of the way and they kept on working. My heart sank. If my leg was broken, no trip for me. I slowly drug myself up and tried to stand on my feet. There would have had to been no less than a thousand pounds rolled up over my feet and legs then driven off. Incredibly nothing was broken. My right leg swelled up so bad that I was afraid I might not get my jeans off. I told my cousins not to say anything because this would just upset everyone. They complied with my request and although my leg was swollen and bruised, my parents never found out about it!

As the year before, haymaking got done and the day of our great trip arrived. The plan was, as soon as my milking chores were done the gang would ride out from the farm. Four of five of the riders showed up and I excitedly but anxiously went into the milking parlor to tell Dad we were leaving. He always was diligent in caressing the cows' udders. This would relax them to release all their milk. He would do this with his head on their flank and was so habitual about it that he would talk with people but rarely look away from his task. If he did, then he had a point to make. I was praying in my heart that he wouldn't look up and just say "be careful". Instead, he asked,

"Have you seen your cow?" During this time my one milk cow, Christy, which I had shown at the fair but not for two years, a cow which now was a herd cow along with the other one hundred head or so of cows, and didn't make me a dime, was due to have a calf. If a cow had a calf back in the pasture, which they did often in the summer, they would stay with their calves, and you would have to herd them separately. It was imperative that you get her into the barn to get her milked or she most likely would get milk fever. Dad knew she was close and hadn't seen her in the herd. My heart dropped. I hadn't even thought of her as "my cow" for all this time and now in the moment before I go to have the greatest time in my life, he drops this on me! I said, " But Dad, the guys are here waiting to go!" His reply only guilted me to go out and tell the gang I couldn't go until I found "my" cow. They looked at me as if I was betraying them. I was so upset! They argued that I should just get on my cycle and ride it out but deep down in my heart I knew what I had to do. As they rode away, I immediately headed for the pasture to find Christy. I walked through all the cows that had been milked or turned out because they were "dry". She wasn't there. I walked through the night-lot with my head and heart swimming, still not believing what was happening to me. Our farm's pasture was huge. Because of the number of cows we had, it took a lot of ground to pasture them all. Much of it was woods as well because you can't farm woods. Needless to say, I didn't find her until I was about as far away from the barn and as deep in the woods as I could get, and to make matters worse, her calf was dead.

I don't remember, but I'm sure I cried. I felt as if I had been hit by a truck. How could my life get any worse. This was the beginning of the greatest pity party of all times, and I was determined to make my Dad feel as bad as I did at that moment. But then something happened. That still, small voice that we all have deep down in our hearts began to whisper things to me. The first thing it said was 'behold this mother standing beside her dead child'. Then I noticed her udder was deep red; a sign of all the swelling from milk produced for a new calf. If she didn't get milked quickly, she was going to be really sick. Normally a calf will be up on its feet in a few minutes and will hungrily suck this milk, releasing the pressure for the cow. This wasn't going to happen, and I needed to get her away from the dead calf and headed towards the barn. She didn't want to leave at first, but I finally got her moving in the right direction as we walked, I had time to listen to that voice in my heart and to reflect on my life and who I was becoming.

Luke15:4NKJV and Mathew18:12NKJV are the same parable told by two different men which heard it from Jesus. "What man of you, having a hundred sheep and one is lost, doesn't leave the ninety-nine in the wilderness to go after that which is lost until he finds it?" I only had one cow in my herd. How could I have become so self-absorbed that I would let her be lost? And what about my best friends? Why hadn't they offered to help look for her or at least wait? The anticipation is always greater than the act. I found out later that I enjoyed that trip much more in my mind visualizing it than they did going on it. They had problems, they fought, and they got rained on a lot. My trip had none of that.

I got Christy into the barn just before the last cow went in. As I got her in the stanchion, Dad look at me with such compassion and asked, "What about the calf?" "It's dead!" is all I said. He just sadly nodded and began to work on Christy. Then he turned and looked at me and said, "You can go and catch up with your friends if you want?" I told him "No, I don't know which way they were going and don't know where they will be stopping to camp." Nothing more was ever said of this trip, but I learned volumes about compassion and responsibility by not going.

Ghosts

A dear young friends father just died. A Godly man of 69. It was unexpected and his son (my friend) is taking it hard. Even though they are both saved, the young man misses his father's daily guidance and talks. I reflect on losing my Dad and I told him he will think about him every day. And that's a good thing. I didn't say anything to him about seeing ghosts, but I know he will. Not the kind of ghosts That are spooky but the kind that when you are in certain places where you and your loved ones frequented a lot or you have really good memories of them there, you will see them not visually but in your heart. Heart memories are the absolute best. I first started seeing Harry when I looked at his recliner where he had spent much of his time in the last few months. He was always relaxed there. That's how I saw him. If I go into his old shop or the milk house, he is there. Every little detail of him springs from my heart and he is there. How he stood. One leg slightly bent. How he smiled or looked up from whatever he might have been doing. Features and characteristics that I have forgotten about Harry will manifest themselves when I see his ghost. Even his clothes and how he smelled can be a part of these apparitions.

Where I see Dad's ghost the best is in the woods. I spend as much time there as I can, and rarely do I go anywhere in our family's woods that I don't see him and sometimes my uncles too! Dad loved to be there as well. He loved to hunt mushrooms so much that I loved it at first just by association, after time, I longed for spring and mushroom season. Now I must say, anymore it is pretty much a waste of time. I don't find anywhere near the number of mushrooms that I used to, but the other benefits of being in the woods make up for it.

Harry taught my brothers and I volumes of knowledge in the woods. One of his first lessons and a very important one was what to do if you got lost. How to get home. Our main woods with the neighbors covers over a thousand acres. In the thick spring undergrowth, a young boy can get separated from his parents very easily as everyone is silently looking for mushrooms. He taught us that if that ever happened (and it did) that we should follow the slope down until we found water, follow it to the creek, then walk upstream until you came out of the woods or knew where you were. This really wasn't an issue for me because I loved staying close to him there. Watching him hunt was a great study and it has helped me be a better hunter as well. He also knew the best spots. He would hunt his way into a patch very methodically, being careful not to miss or worse, step on any mushrooms. Once he got to a prime spot, he would stop, lean onto his 'walking stick' and slowly scan the ground from that vantage point until he was sure he hadn't missed any, then move a few steps to his next point. What excitement I would feel when I heard his soft whistle. That was his announcement that he had found one. Everyone within hearing distance would perk up and start looking harder. Us kids would start heading his way and were reprimanded if we weren't careful in watching our steps. It would be a 'sin' to crush a mushroom under your foot. We knew Dad wasn't going to pick any until we got there and that he was going to let us pick the ones we could see standing beside him, but the sooner you got there, the more time you had to see them. " One... two... threee ... fourrr. ". He would softly and slowly count out loud all that he was seeing, drawing out the numbers as he looked. Talk about making your heartbeat! Once everyone got there that was coming, and had time to view what he saw, he would stand there and direct us to any we hadn't seen, and he wouldn't pick any himself until he was sure we had picked all that he had seen. After he was sure all to be found were found, he would casually move on to the next patch. This taught me patience and persistence.

He taught us about the trees and plants when we weren't finding any mushrooms. He knew every species there was and delighted in showing what made them unique, one from another. What trees made the best firewood and how they rotted once they died. Some like Shagbark Hickory wouldn't last a year on the ground so you would want to cut it quicker so it wouldn't go to waste. Others like Walnut could lay for years in the woods and still be fine for firewood. Often times there would be a history lesson thrown in about certain things that had happened when he was a kid in the places we were in, and he had names for these spots which echoed back to a time I would never know but could imagine about. "Dutch Davey had a tree fall on him over there when we were logging. Could have killed him but just broke his leg really bad. That's why he limps. We had to carry him out by hand." "This low draw through here is the tobacco patch. It still grew wild here when I was a kid." "Your Grandma used to pick paw paws here."

The best place, for me, to see his ghost in the woods is a place called Donnie's Rock. After you have worked through some thick undergrowth and up a ravine, there, in a stand of hickories, on top of another deep ravine, sits Donnie's Rock. This boulder is at least five feet by five feet and twenty to thirty inches high. It is fairly flat on top and the perfect place to stop and sit. Oftentimes, this is where Mom would feed us the picnic she had toted in while hunting mushrooms. It wouldn't be much more than bologna sandwiches but after hunting for a few hours, that was enough. Mom would always say "Donnie Fawcett always came home from hunting mushrooms with the biggest bags full. He always said this place is where he found them". That would cause my father to tell us other stories about Donnie and other old men who had frequented these woods and passed. We wouldn't stay there long. But by the time we had ate and visited, we would be ready to hunt our way out of the woods.

Donnie's Rock is a mystery to me. There are no other boulders or rocks like it around. It is as if it had been placed there, but due to its massive size, I can't think that any men put it there. God could. The Bible makes reference to memorials set up by men to never forget what had happened in those places, but Donnie's Rock doesn't fit with them. What does fit is what the Bible tells us about the Holy Spirit. 1st Corinthians 2:12-16NKJV tells us: "Now we have received, not the spirit of the world, but the spirit which is of God; that we might know the things that are freely given to us of God. Which things we also speak, not in the words which man's wisdom teaches, but which the Holy Ghost teaches, comparing spiritual things with spiritual. But the natural man receives not the things of the Spirit of God, for they are foolishness unto him, neither can he know them, because they are spiritually discerned. But he that is spiritual judges all things, yet he himself is judged of no man. For whom hath known the mind of the Lord, that he may instruct him? But we have the mind of Christ."

The Holy Spirit, or the Holy Ghost, is mentioned hundreds of times in the Bible. All true believers in Christ know the Holy Ghost because he is Jesus, and God's gift to us. He guides us and empowers us to be "children of God". He is Christ in us! I know that nonbelievers would say I'm out of my mind for saying I see ghosts, but what they don't know is, I don't see dead people, but the peace and joy and hope that only comes from loving God. What comfort and joy I find knowing that those beautiful times and people at Donnie's Rock will go on for eternity. I pray thank you to God for giving my young friend the same Holy Spirit to see and remember with joy the ghost of his father the same way I see mine.

My grandson Owen at Donnie's Rock

Happy Birthday Donnie

The Holy Spirit has a very subtle yet profound way of bringing to my memory events and people from my past that make up who I am. He has gently nudged me into writing about Donn Fawcett. I tell myself, "This book is about my Dad Harry." but, the Spirit leads me to know that a certain few people are a garnishment to that story.

I got a text from Bob (another person who has been so much to me in my life) that today would have been Donnie's 132nd birthday. Donnie was Bob's grandfather. He is also the man behind the story of Donnie's Rock, but there is so much more to him in my life than that.

Donnie was a big man and gruff. His apparel was always the same, bib overalls and a flannel or denim work shirt. His eyes belied his gruff nature. And gravelly voice. His scary demeanor was accentuated by ever present tobacco stains at the corners of his mouth. I think he always had a chew in his mouth. I was in awe of him, mesmerized by him, but not afraid of him.

My most profound memory of Donnie was the last time I saw him. I was five years old. I don't know why I needed a babysitter that day, but Aunt Ruth was watching me. Mom rarely needed a babysitter, but Aunt Ruth was always there for the task. There were only three of us there that day as all the older kids were in school and my sister Jill was only a couple of months old. I think that mom had taken her to the doctor. Aunt Ruth, Donnie and me. I vaguely remember feeling privileged to have Donnie all to myself and he really did the babysitting because I wouldn't leave him alone or vice versa.

Sometime in the afternoon, Aunt Ruth decided we needed a nap. She took me to her and Uncle Bruce's bedroom and made me lie down with her. The house was very still and within minutes Aunt Ruth was asleep.

Having no desire to sleep at all, I gently removed myself from the bedroom. My hope was that Donnie would be awake but as I made my way down the hall, I could hear him snoring.

That in itself was a show worth watching. I sat down on the couch across from his chair and was mesmerized by the rhythmic, guttural snoring. It was loud and I waited patiently for him to wake himself up.

I don't know how long I watched, but at a point, his breathing changed for just a few seconds, then his head rolled forward and tobacco juice ran from his mouth. Since this didn't startle him awake, I felt something was wrong. I anxiously went to Aunt Ruth and woke her up. I know I surprised her to be off the bed shaking her. She asked me if I was alright and I told her "Yeah, but I think something is wrong with Donnie." She was quick at getting up and getting to his chair. I was right behind her. In that short distance, I had a few thoughts. "Was I going to be in trouble for not taking a nap? Would I be in trouble for waking Aunt Ruth? Or Donnie?" But mostly, "What is happening here?"

Aunt Ruth tried waking him, but to no avail. She became frantic then very upset crying and pleading with Donnie to wake up. I don't know when she called for the ambulance, but I just wanted to be away from this drama. I started to go outside, and Ruth said, "Oh Joey, please don't run away!" I said I wouldn't and stood on the porch until the ambulance came.

What a different world than what we live in today. There were no cell phones. The township fire department was on a land line at someone's house. They would in turn call volunteers to go to the firehouse to get the ambulance which wasn't much more than a station wagon with a gurney. The volunteers had very little equipment that went with their very little training, so the biggest part of their job was to comfort Ruth and move Donnie onto his bed. I'm sure they contacted the funeral home and walked Ruth through what needed to be done.

When Bob and Susan got off the bus, I was waiting there on the front porch. Bob came running up excited to see me and ready to play but I ruined that by telling them that Donnie died. Susan, who was probably 9 at the time began crying and ran into the house. Bob was a little more controlled and walked in with me. We all loved Donnie and grieved in our own way, but I remember standing over his lifeless body with Bob and I talking with subdued voices. This was a place and situation that neither one of us had been in before. We had seen pets, livestock, and wild animals die but not a person. Not anyone close. There was a great peace there in Donnie's room.

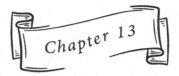

The Accident

As I prayed this morning, not thinking at all about writing, the Holy Spirit put this chapter in my heart. I was praying about issues that my grandchildren are having to deal with in their lives right now and after He gave me great insight into those issues, He brought me back to this story which in many ways reflects on what one grandson is going through.

Guilt is a sword of the devil. He tries to make us feel guilty when often times we are not. When we are guilty of something it is the thing that should cause us to repent and turn back to Jesus. The most important thing is no matter where or how guilt manifests itself, whether we are guilty or not, Jesus is the only answer to remove it. He has already paid the price for it on the cross.

One cold, wintery Saturday, we were hauling or spreading manure. Yes, that job is just as detestable as it sounds. I always thought it ironic that all summer long we hauled hay and straw into the barns just to turn around and haul it out in the fall, winter, and spring in its recycled state. It isn't hard work, but it doesn't matter about the weather, but when we had time to haul manure, that's what we did. All day long, load after load, from barn to field. On cold days you may run into the milk house and stand in front of the space heater to warm up while Dad filled your 'spreader', but it was best if you wore enough clothes to stay warm and maybe just carefully go in where he was loading you out. It's amazing how much warmer it can be just inside an unheated barn. As Dad would dig out the mixture of straw and cow manure, steam would often times roll out of the exposed inner layer to the point you couldn't see through the fog. It would be clearly twenty degrees warmer near this eruption and even though it was very odorous, it felt good.

Dad was the only one that loaded manure outside of allowing us boys to try our hand at it occasionally. He was a master. His loader was an older 77 Oliver with a narrow front end or 'row crop'. It had a simple John Deere loader mounted on it. The two hydraulic cylinders that did the lifting were run by a pump that was directly connected to the power takeoff of the tractor. The actual dumping of the manure from the bucket was done by pulling a trip lever. The weight of the load would cause the bucket to pivot over, dumping its load. Once gravity had caused the manure to fall out, two springs would pull the bucket back to the locked position. This tractor had no power steering and no automatic transmission. Dad's left foot ran the clutch. His right foot worked the brakes but more importantly, his left hand ran the hoist and drove while his right hand shifted gears, ran the throttle, tripped the bucket, and did the major part of steering using a steering knob that was attached to the steering wheel. Half of his driving was in reverse. Inside barns were posts and tight spaces, yet he did it as if he had eyes in the back of his head. We had one barn (the calf pens) where the top of the door opening was so low that he would have to lean over to be lower than the steering wheel so he wouldn't get knocked off when he drove in. Once he was in, he could raise back up. It used to drive me mad with worry, thinking he would forget just once to lean over as he backed out. It would have taken just once to kill him. He was poetry in motion, no wasted movements. Even how he speared into the manure was calculated. It had to be picked apart. The loader could only lift so much, and Dad knew how to methodically do it. I believe he felt the same joy and satisfaction doing this as a concert pianist feels playing a major musical piece. That may be a little over the top but not much. It compelled us 'haulers' to do our best to keep up.

This particular day, as I pulled out of the cow lot at Uncle John's barn and prepared to pull out on county road 5, my Aunt Ruth pulled up in front of Grampa's house, which was right across the road. Cousin Bob jumped out of the car and came running to see me. We were closer than twins in those days. He was my best friend and companion, and I was overjoyed to see him. This was the last load of the day and once I got it off, I would drive back to our barn and do chores during milking to finish the day. It was a given that he was going to ride with me to the field but as he climbed up on the tractor, I slid off the seat and said "You drive. I've been driving all day". Without pause, he was on the seat and pulling out on the road. Bob had driven tractors all his life like me, so this wasn't unusual for him to be driving. I was completely at ease riding with him. So much so that I was right in his ear talking about everything that two fourteen- or fifteen-year-old friends who hadn't seen each other for a few days needed to talk about. I was standing on a step which was right on the rear axle of the tractor. This put me on the same eye level as Bob. I was leaning on the fender of the large rear tire and holding on to a light mount. This was a very common method of riding on this 1954 Oliver 77. After going about a quarter of a mile, we drove past Uncle John's house, where county road 5 takes a slight curve to the left and descends quite a bit. I remember looking ahead and there wasn't a vehicle to be seen for the half mile you could see ahead. 200 more yards and we began to turn left into the field I had been pulling into all day but as I kept talking, Bob looked back. I saw a look of terror come into his eyes. As I quickly spun to see his fear, I just caught a glimpse of a pickup truck as it crashed into the wheel on which I was leaning.

That point of impact was so quick, so powerful that I lost all control of my body and what it was going through. Even as quick as it was, I remember a lot of the details as if it were slow motion. The impact knocked me off between the tractor and the spreader. My right cheek bone slammed into the top front frame of the spreader. Instantly, I was under the spreader. The momentum of the impact caused the spreader, truck, and tractor to keep moving down the road. The distance between the spreader and the road was not much more than 12 inches and my body was rolled and ground head over heels like a rag doll. I remember my head smacking the road and out of the corner of my eye, I saw the spreader tire coming right toward my head. Something caused my head and body to jerk up and forward then slam right back down. At that instant... everything had stopped. My head was resting ON the wheel. I passed out. I don't know how long I was out but when I came to, there was total silence. I was immediately filled with quilt. I just knew that I was the only one who had lived through this horrific crash. I prayed that God would forgive me for causing this wreck that had to have killed my best friend and others. Why did I have to distract Bob as he was driving. I should have been driving. I prayed again and felt some peace as I realized I was probably not hurt too bad. I finally got the nerve to call out. "Bob?" I heard feet shuffling then saw shadows out from under the spreader where I laid. Then I hear this sobbing voice say, "Are you alive?" Another quick prayer "Thank you Jesus, this one's alive". "Are you hurt bad?" he asked. "I don't think so." I told him "Where's Bob?" "He ran up the road to get help." "Is anyone else hurt?" I asked, expecting to hear the worst. As he told me his little brother had received a goose egg of a bump on his forehead, but that I was the worst. I began to assess how bad I was. My right cheek felt as if it had been hit with a hammer. I slowly worked down my body and was relieved to see I was pretty much intact except for scrapes and bruises and one ankle that hurt like my face. I remember the young driver murmuring and sobbing, repeating how glad he was that I was alive. I believe he was trying to comfort me even though he needed it more. I slowly began pulling myself out from under this five-ton load of manure and steel and wasn't completely out when the local volunteer rescue squad pulled up. As they examined me and put an air cast on my ankle, I heard a familiar sound it took me a moment to realize what it was but as they lifted me onto the stretcher, I realized that it was Dad, on the loader. I was flooded with more quilt and emotion because what I knew was that the word that had gotten to him was that I had been in a bad wreck and was under the spreader. He, in his mind, saw me trapped, possibly suffocating, under the load and that the only chance of getting me out was the loader. It was the slowest tractor we had, and I can't imagine the fear he felt getting there. I saw his face as they rolled me into the ambulance, and he looked almost disappointed that he couldn't help.

Over the years I have come to believe that he felt the greatest quilt because I was working for him when this happened. My quilt hung heavy with me for the next few days as I lay in the hospital. I knew Bob must hate me. He was having to deal with this accident while I was being treated like royalty in bed. Finally, Aunt Ruth brought him to the hospital to see me. As he walked into the room, we both burst into tears. "Oh Bobby, I'm so sorry." I cried out. He said, "You're sorry? I almost killed you. I'm sorry"

What a relief I felt to confess my guilt, whether real or imagined, and to find Bob was going through the same thing. I hope I remember right that he felt the same relief. As we talked about the wreck, Bob revealed to me what his experience was. Like me, he too was saved from death by God's grace. The tractor, on impact, broke into three main pieces. I would guess that no one piece weighed less than eight hundred pounds. He found himself pinned to the road by the tractor hitch which was buried two or three inches into the pavement. One third of the tractor's weight, came down on this two inch by three inch by eight inch long piece of hardened steel, grazing his arm just inches from his head.

Jeremiah 29:11 answers the question I've asked myself a thousand times over the years. God, why did you keep us from being killed?

The NLT version says it best. "For I know the plans I have for you" says the Lord. "They are plans for good and not disaster. To give you a future and a hope."

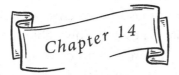

Married to Cows

This Sunday morning, I'm sitting in a hospital room on the twentieth floor of the James Cancer Hospital in Columbus. This last month has been a roller coaster ride of emotional ups and downs, testing both my wife Debbie's and my faith. I will not go into details but explain that Debbie was diagnosed with ovarian cancer and this past Thursday underwent major surgery and now is trying to recover enough to start chemotherapy. I will also say that our Savior has kept us at peace with this that goes beyond understanding.

As a nurse was tending to Deb, their conversation turned to fields being flooded with water and Deb stated that the poor farmers were the biggest gamblers. My mind raced back to when my Dad and uncles had to gamble, or at least had to let the dice fall where they may. The truth of the matter is the Bible says in Jeremiah 29:11 NKJV: "For I know the plans I have for you, declares the LORD. Plans to prosper you and not to harm you, plans to give you hope and a future." It takes good faith to know that is true and wisdom has taught me through the years that He will see us through all calamities. The term "Let go and let GOD" seems really appropriate to our situation now as it did back to the days on the farm.

One spring afternoon as we waited on Uncle Bud to bring the cows in for milking, Jack and I became concerned as the time had passed when they should have been up. They began to appear at the back of the night lot, but it didn't take long to discern that something wasn't right. Some of them were staggering. Some were changing directions radically, and some of them would just stop and stand in one spot even though Bud was yelling and hitting them to move. It was easy to tell that Bud was completely rattled by the situation. Jack and I instinctively drove the front, more normal acting cows, in and started milking. We explained to Dad the best we could to what was going on and he rushed out to help Bud and to assess the situation. Our once normal and mundane task of milking turned into a nightmare. It would have been distressing to have one cow acting so abnormal, but this was insanity. We had no more got the milkers on one cow, and she dropped dead right there. It took quite a bit of effort to get her out of the stanchion and drug out of the milking parlor so another one could come in to be milked. With milk cows you can't call a timeout even in the most severe situations. You have to get them milked or several things can happen to them which are not good. If they don't get milk fever or mastitis, which is bad, they will just stop producing milk and milk is the end product that makes dairying viable.

A milk cow is either making you money or costing you. There isn't any in between. In all dairy cows' lives there comes a time when they are no longer profitable, so you sell them. This is the normal process. A cow will start producing milk after giving birth to her first calf at around two years of age. She can produce milk for up to ten years, taking out the time she is "dried up" and producing a calf. Our herd always had a bull with them so when it came time for a cow to breed and have another calf, it came naturally and in its own season. Having a bull with the herd also kept the numbers stable and production relatively the same week to week. What we were dealing with this evening was catastrophic. Sometime during trying to milk a bunch of mad cows and pulling dead or incapacitated cows out of the way, the vet was called. By the time he got there, we had pretty much got the ones milked that could be milked and found ourselves standing uncertainly in the middle of what looked like a massacre. I never saw my Dad look so worried and can't imagine how he made it through the night not knowing what would be left of his herd come morning.

Doc Irwin, the vet, determined that the cows had eaten leaves off young Buckeye trees. It's a rare thing that they do this. Nobody knew why they did this spring, but the aftermath was nine cows dead, sixteen so sick they would never produce again, and all the milk dumped down the drain for two weeks due to the toxicity of the buckeye leaves. One fourth of the herd was gone. We spent every chance we got cutting and burning Buckeye trees for a long time.

Brother Bill, who had recently come home from Colorado to visit, and as I asked him or Jack to share their memories on these events, he reminded me that our heifers (young cows, not yet milking) had on the very same day, ate Buckeye leaves too!! In another woods.

I'm sure no one saw the plan God had for us at the time but now, fifty some years later, at least I can look back on this tragic event and see how true Jeremiah 29:11 is. My family moved on from this event almost as if it never happened. Outside of all the extra hard work of killing Buckeye saplings, our lifestyle never changed, but deep within our collective family psyche we gained more than we could ask for. Fifty or so years later, all thirteen cousins are still alive. All thirteen grew up to be strong and independent. We are a very blessed family. We don't know what the future holds but are continually filled with hope and a certainty that God is in control.

If you are old enough and lived in Ohio, you will remember the blizzard of 78. All you have to say to someone over fifty is 'blizzard of 78' and you will create a conversation of competitive recollections of how bad it was. If you don't know about it, just google it. You will see that most of the incredible stories you hear are true. I don't try to compete in these story battles because I know what I know, and I know what Dad went through for the cows.

I will relate my personal story to perhaps better develop Dad's story. One that I can't ever remember him telling anyone how bad it was, but that was his nature.

The evening before the storm was incredibly warm and rainy, especially for late in January. It was in the 60's. The wind gradually picked up and by one o'clock there were gale force winds. I looked out at our barn where forty heifers were bedded and saw the two large main doors flapping in the wind. Each door was approximately sixteen feet high and at least ten feet wide. They were normally wired shut but the wire had broken and now if it wasn't for their rollers on top being inside their channel rails, they would have flown away like two large kites. I feared this would happen and knew that I needed to get them stabilized and shut for the safety of the cows and to preserve the doors. After making my way out there, I found that if I tried pushing the doors down at the bottom to the closed position, another blast of wind would come and blow the door straight out parallel to the ground, shoving me away like a ragdoll. I devised a plan to throw enough bales out of the mow and stack them in front of the doors until the weight would keep them closed. This was no easy task. I would get ten or so bales in front of one of the doors and then the wind would cause the door to scatter them away. Slowly, adding more bales, I finally got them shut.

I had over fifty bales out in front of the doors before I could rewire them shut and hope the combination would hold. Completely worn out, I made my way to the house. I was no more inside than the power went out. I crawled into bed with both Deb and our oldest daughter, Amy, knowing I better try to get some much-needed rest now because I was going to be busy later trying to keep us warm. I may have slept three or four hours only to wake up to the sound of a roaring train blowing around (and through) our old house. I noticed that a snow drift had formed under our television. Our house was very old and was almost impossible to heat in good times. Now I feared for my wife and daughter and prayed we wouldn't freeze. Any thought of escaping to a warmer place was squelched by the knowledge that I couldn't take a two-year-old and a pregnant mother out in a storm that you couldn't see ten feet in. We pretty much spent the next two days covered up in bed, waiting for some reprieve from the storm.

On the third day, I decided I had to go to the barn to check on the heifers. It was my responsibility to take care of these young cows and I knew how important that was. Dad had taught me that. I also worried for him, the rest of my family, and the main herd as it could be no better for them. Those cows had to be milked! Had Dad been able to make it to the barn? Were the cows still alive? When I reached the barn and peered in, my heart sank. It was nothing but solid white. I immediately assumed that snow was three to four feet deep everywhere in the barn. Certainly, all the heifers had either froze to death or suffocated under the snow. Then I noticed a crack in the snow and as I stared at it, I saw some slight movement. It was as if the floor came alive. All around I noticed more movement. Even though the heifers were pretty much buried they seemed quite content lying under the insulation of the snow. My appearance had startled them enough to get them moving and after a while, I realized they were all alive. There was nothing I could do or needed to do for them, so l made my way back into the house. This storm had dropped more than twenty inches of snow and the temperature had plunged from a balmy 50-60 degrees to a minus 40 below zero chill factor in just hours. Even though it had quit snowing, the strong winds still made visibility difficult.

I don't remember if it was cabin fever, worry about my Dad or the cows, or just curiosity, but I decided it was time I walked to the milk barn to assess the damage and see what I could do to help. The main barn is only about 11/2 miles from our house as a crow fly and I promised Deb if it looked too treacherous, I would turn around and come home. Dad had taught me well on how to protect my body in the cold. I knew that any exposed skin could become frostbit in minutes in this weather and everything needed to be covered. As I left the house the only thing you could see was my eyes. I was sure I wasn't going to get too cold because it was taking so much effort to move through the snow. Some places were deep and crusty snow. Some places were bare frozen ground. The wind had created drifts that allowed me to walk right over fences and ditches, which could have been problematic in normal storms but now it was a new landscape. Most of the time my eyes could only look straight down to keep them clear, occasionally looking up to make sure I was headed in the right direction. About two thirds of the way there, as I was squinting, looking down, I noticed a perfectly round, black object on the ground. I immediately stopped and through the blowing snow around my feet, I began to bend down to see what it was. I almost had a heart attack as the snow cleared long enough to realize that what I was looking at was a patch of asphalt, a spot of county road 5, twelve to fifteen feet below me. The top of this hole was maybe ten feet across and looking down in it was like looking into a very steep sided funnel. I don't know what would have happened if I had taken one more step. I can only believe that the Holy Spirit had me open my eyes at the exact moment I needed to see this abyss. Maybe I could have dug and climbed out of there, but I strongly doubt it. This section of road had a high bank on it, and it was over two weeks before the county highway department was able to clear it with heavy equipment.

To my relief, as I neared the milk house, I heard a tractor running. It wasn't moving but turning the portable generator to produce the electricity needed to run everything in the barn and Uncle Bud's house. That meant there were cows to be milked and someone to do it. I walked into the milk house and as I tried to recover from my trek and get some of my clothes off, I noticed every piece of Tupperware and glass jar Aunt Lib owned filled with milk. There was also a small stream of milk running from the bulk tank to the floor drain. There was nothing left to do but let it go down the drain until the milk truck could come to pick it up. I don't remember how long that took, but at least the cows were able to be milked.

I said a prayer as I walked into the milking parlor. "Please God, let Dad be here." In Ohio, fifty-one people died in that blizzard. I didn't know that at the time, but I did know Harry's resolve. I knew his top priority would be to get to the barn not only for the cows' sake, but for his brother's too. Once I saw him, I was filled with relief. He had a way of milking that was so calming to the cow that it would calm you down just watching. His head was always nestled in her flank and one or both of his hands would be massaging their udders. I think Bud was more surprised to see me than Dad and excitedly welcomed me and pressed me about my journey. Dad just casually turned his head where he could see me and gave me a soft smile. One thing about Harry, he could speak a thousand words with how he looked at you. What he told me, with his eyes, that day was "You are the man that I raised you to be. You know how to survive in the worst storm. You know how to protect yourself from the elements and I'm not at all surprised that you're here to help." After that, I enjoyed the blizzard, knowing that all was well with my family and the herd. Knowing that I was becoming more like him every day. Knowing that we had survived this storm.

Water Skiing

Dad did very few things for his own joy or entertainment, at least not of the physical kind. He worked so hard that when he found a moment to relax, he relaxed! In that, he taught us boys a very valuable lesson. Power napping. It is something that is not talked about or written about but is a very effective way to rejuvenate a tired body. I have seen it used by other industrious people over the years and when confronted about it, everyone that does it proudly proclaims its benefits. Every day after lunch or "dinner" as we knew it, Dad would go to his recliner, push back and within a few minutes would be asleep. I found this always amazing, but over time, I saw first Bill, then Jack do the same thing. Dad would wake up fifteen minutes later as if he had slept for eight hours. As soon as he folded his recliner up my brothers would wake up as well and out the door we would go back to work.

I suppose I started doing it because I got bored watching the three of them sleeping, but once I found out how refreshing it was, I followed suit. If visitors came to our house at that time, they would see us strung out all over the place. Dad in his chair, Bill or Jack on the couch and me and the other brother usually on the floor, porch, or yard. Years later, I walked into construction sites where I found builders strung out, doing this very same thing.

We are blessed to have several Amish builders in our community, and they are specifically adept at this practice. There are several places in the Bible where this practice is supported. Hebrews chapter 4 covers it best for me, but we all know the story of Jesus going into the stern of the boat and sleeping when the ship came into a storm. After Jesus calmed the wind and the sea, He rebuked his disciples for not having enough faith. To be able to rest or "nap" like this is deeply rooted in the faith that God keeps us through it all. He rested on the seventh day, not that God needed to, but to teach us that principle.

I, once again, went on a tangent. It is important to know how valuable rest and relaxation are to the human spirit. Dad found a great reward in giving in to frivolity one Sunday afternoon. Mom's youngest brother Bobby, who with his wife and kids visited us often, told Dad that he had gotten into water skiing. His enthusiasm for the sport was so great that he aroused Dad's curiosity and in a short time, convinced Dad to try it.

The very next Sunday found us traveling north to an old, abandoned gravel pit which over time had turned into a lake. It's gravel base allowed backing a boat trailer into it to launch a motorboat. Uncle Bobby was both instructor and captain and did a wonderful job at both. I don't remember much about that day, only that Dad was a natural at it and loved every aspect of it. But most importantly, Dad had lived most of his life with a bad back. It could have been from his injuries from the war or some accident on the farm. I had never known him not wearing a back brace even when he slept. And though it was not his nature to complain, I saw him hurting so bad that he would literally crawl to the bathroom during his worst times. Well, that all changed after that one day of skiing. To him it was nothing short of a miracle. After years of going to chiropractors to no avail, he found relief in the pain. We spent every Sunday afternoon the rest of that summer going to that old pit. Poor Uncle Bobby spent most of his time just pulling Dad around that pit. He did teach us boys how to do it so he got some reprieve and I know he couldn't be happier or prouder that he had done so much to change Dad's life.

Way before it was spring, Dad was on a mission. He sought out and found a ski boat. It was terribly dated but was very capable of doing what Dad needed it to do. We called it the bat boat because it had tail fins like a '57 Chevy, like Batman's boat on tv. It had a fifty-horse Evinrude motor which was capable of pulling two skiers. It also could easily pull one man on a single ski and since that was what Dad had learned to do, and enjoyed so much the previous summer, it made it perfect!

Most people who own boats take great pride in keeping them looking nice. I've seen people spend as much time cleaning and waxing them as actually riding in them. Not Harry. His only concern was that it was fast and powerful enough to ski with. He did buy rubbing compound that we buffed the old red (which had faded pink) hull with and it did look some better. He spent all his free time in the spring prepping and tweaking the motor so it would be ready to go the first warm Sunday that came.

The drive to the Dunkirk quarry took thirty to forty-five minutes. Coupled with the drive back and getting ready to milk only left a precious hour or two for Dad to ski. The last time I remember that we skied there was on Labor Day 1967. It was cold and rainy but was a very special day as brother Bill was home on furlough from the Army and left the very next day for Vietnam. Looking back on it now, I can only imagine how anxious Dad must have been about that day. Bill had been away training and had never shared in Dad's newfound pleasure. I'm sure Dad wanted those few hours to be very special because, more than any of the rest of us, he knew what kind of peril Bill was going to be stepping into. His memory of being in war was as acute as if he had just got out himself. This might be the last thing he ever did with his oldest son. I thank God that it wasn't.

Through that fall and winter, Dad mentioned occasionally that he believed we could ski on the pond. Our pond, which we built in 1962-63, is three acres big. Shaped in a rectangle where it is about three times as long as it is wide. I guess you could say it's a lake by its size but not much more than a pond. It's a beautiful place where I loved to fish and hunt, but to ski on? I thought Dad had gone completely mad. I think others thought so too but when spring rolled around, Harry was determined to give it a try.

The first step was to see if we could get "the Bat boat" up to speed without running ashore. You had to basically be turning the whole time, running in an elliptical pattern. Moss and frogs and everything else in the shallow edge water washed up into the trees that grew along the edge. I found it somewhat amusing and figured Dad would realize that this may not be a good idea as much of the time, if that worked, he would be skiing in pretty shallow water. Water where you could see the old tree stumps only inches under the surface. Later in the summer, when the water level was down, I would jump out on these to fish. Nevertheless, Dad decided to try it. He shortened the tow rope up, jumped in the ole mossy pond, and yelled his favorite line "Let her happen Cap'n." I don't recall who was driving but I think it was brother Jack. Harry started out with two skis as it doesn't take as much speed to ski with two. He was not long in kicking one off and the rest is history. Harry could now ski twice as long as when he was going to the quarry and every Sunday found him and mom and whoever else he could get to join him in his sport. I never cared to do it but many of his friends did, and the picnics were the best!

Neither of Dad's brothers were interested in it at all. I think they may have thought that it wasn't good for the pond initially, but what we found out, it kept it cleaner and not so weedy due to the agitation of the old Bat boat. The pond was built to be a source of water for our dairy herd so the few times that they used it, they didn't need to wade out to get a drink like they would have if cattails took over the shallow water. We still had cattails but only at one end.

Dad's final quest in waterskiing was the 'piece de resistance' of his sport. He had decided that he could make a ski jump and over the next winter he designed the thing and built it. It was like watching a slow train wreck. In my mind, I was hoping and expecting him to come to the realization that it was going to take too much time and effort to construct something that would probably kill you in the end. He had no knowledge of what was involved in ski jumping ramps. He may have seen one on tv but there was no technical support to call on in its construction. Dad had built a lot of things over the years and his fabrications, in the end, always were a benefit to the farm. But almost all his inventions had to be modified from their original form to work; sometimes modified several times. This was different. You only had one shot at it, or you were going to get hurt or killed. He didn't have a coach to tell him what to do or how to protect himself. He was on his own in this endeavor. Every step in the process, I thought, would bring him to his senses, but no. I mentioned earlier that Dad was fearless and usually full of common sense but this time, no. I didn't argue with him about this. I had too much respect for him to do that and honestly I had learned that he was always right when I did think I knew more than him. I just stayed away from him and this venture whenever he was working on it.

In the end, he had managed to get this contraption back to the pond and in it. He had welded brackets on a large cylindrical boiler tank and attached two twelve to sixteen feet long saplings on either side of the tank. On top of those he attached plywood. It was moored to the bank with clothesline rope in the front and rear. It looked somewhat like a half-sunk pontoon boat. The day of reckoning came. I went, not because I wanted to see my Dad die but, to be an able body to drag him to shore if need be. We all watched fearfully as he approached the ramp. It was like watching Evil Knievel making one of his historic motorcycle jumps. The moment Dad hit the ramp he was jerked out of his skis and the tow rope was jerked out of his hands. He literally dived into the ramp and water at the same time. All of us who were on the shore jumped up and ran to save him. Before we could get to him, he surfaced and shouted, "I need to get it wet first". He put both skis back on, grabbed the tow rope and as he came back around, he splashed water on the ramp. He did this twice. As I was saying a silent prayer, Dad came around and flew over the ramp perfectly! He did it several times before anyone else would try it but eventually a couple of his skiing friends did it as well.

Ecclesiastes 3 tells us that 'for everything there is a season and a time for every purpose under the heavens.' I don't know why Dad quit skiing. I'm sure just going around in circles became boring over time. I think he found it hard to get anyone to drive the boat after a while as well. Regardless, the boat went into the shed we had built for it. After a while, some younger people who had skied with Dad ended up with the boat and Dad's back seemed to stay good for the rest of his life. The ski jump became a tilted dock that you could fish from but over time it too 'gave up the ghost.' Dad, in his quiet manner, removed it from the pond and now those joyful Sunday afternoons are barely a memory to us who shared the experience with him.

Life Goes On

I haven't written for a long time. Regardless, I have thought about Dad almost every day. I see things he made or fixed still doing their jobs. Sometimes, like the Holy Spirit, my memory of him checks me into not doing things I shouldn't. Sometimes I wonder how he would deal with issues in my life or how he would react to the many and varied people I encounter. His goodness still permeates our family. Jill, Jack, Bill, Mom and I are all still very close at heart. We may not see or speak to each other often, but it is not necessary to our love for one another and family. It permeates through our spouses, into our children, and right on into our grandchildren.

Recently a local business owner called me, looking for some land. He called me for two reasons. The first of which, as I was the zoning inspector in our township for many years and had helped him to get his property properly zoned, he knows I know all the landowners and what might be available. Secondly, he said that since Roberts's had a lot of ground that maybe we might be willing to sell some. In my heart I knew that probably wasn't going to happen and after we hung up it got me to thinking. Fred and Bertha Roberts have thirteen grandchildren. All thirteen are still alive. All of us, except for Bill, live within fifteen miles from the homestead. Of all the land that we were brought up on, it is all still in the family. When I consider all the real estate that my siblings, cousins, and all our children have acquired over the past years, we have more than doubled the original family homestead.

Psalms 103:13 and 17 NKJV says, "The Lord is like a father to his children, tender and compassionate to those who fear him. But the love of the Lord remains forever with those who fear him. His salvation extends to his children's children."

I tell of our lands not to be prideful. No one in our family is so smart or savvy to acquire what we have on our own. First, God gave our elders the increase, then our parents extended that increase to us by their love and fear of the Lord. I have no doubt that this will continue if we give God the glory for all we are and have.

August 7th, 2021 would be Dad's 99th birthday. My sister Jill has texted the whole family to come to her and Mike's house for a cookout and birthday party for him. Sadly, Dad never met any of his great grandchildren as they weren't born yet. Even sadder is that none of them got to meet him but the greatest testament is that everyone from Phoebe, Linus and Finn, the youngest to Gramma June, the oldest at 94, will try to be there to celebrate him and the legacy he left behind. Twenty years after his death, he is still blessing us all.

How A Man Dies

On my father's ninety fifth birthday, I don't know why, but it made me think of his death. Probably because I have been thinking about his father's death, or maybe because it is also Purple Heart Day, which is a war medal that he got by almost dying. We are all appointed once to die, and my fearless father knew that. Dad didn't fear death, but he did fear getting Alzheimer's. You see, when his father went through that, Dad saw how Grampa deteriorated to someone so much less than what he had been in life. Grampa Fred had been a great student in life. Even though he had never been to college, he had a great command of figures and words. He could remember everything and would astonish people with this ability. He could quote much of the Bible and other writings verbatim. He could work math problems in his head with ease. Fred was also very creative and imaginative. He wrote songs and poems and was constantly filling us grandkids with tales that were so vivid that even though we knew they weren't true, they seemed to be. I think my Dad and Aunt Ruth had a greater appreciation of these skills than the other family members and even though I don't remember Dad ever bragging about Grampa's skills, I saw how he reacted with the slightest smile when Fred performed. What Alzheimer's did to Grampa broke my Dad's heart. Fred did things during this time that were so beneath his character. Losing his memory was tolerable for Dad to experience but how it changed his character and actions were sad and humiliating. It so affected my Dad that he feared it would do the same thing to him. Dad spent the rest of his life trying to prevent this.

Dad recognized that the progression of this disease began with short term memory loss. He began to notice that he couldn't remember names. He would apologize by saying things like "awe I know this" or other condescending things about himself. He began his own regimen of self-improvement by reading anything he could on memory loss, doing word puzzles, reading other things, but mostly by just "staying in the game." He prepared without much notice to us, for his final days, whether he would be disabled mentally or not.

He wanted his affairs in order. He never withdrew from people (at least to my knowledge) and stayed happy and active in his everyday life.

Very early after his Dad had died, Dad picked out his headstone. He and Mom were out in Colorado visiting Brother Bill, when on a sightseeing trip, he noticed a large chunk of marble off the side of the road. They were driving into the very small village named Marble, and it was soon apparent to Dad that this name fit perfectly as most of the homes had marble foundations. Bill explained that this was a mining town from which this marble was used to make most of the monuments and memorials in Washington, D.C. Dad found a book on this in a local gift shop. It was filled with pictures and history of this special town and marble that came out of it. He decided that this was what he wanted for a headstone. He knew that there were several large waste chunks that could be used, and he knew that there were several stone cutters who could perform the task of making Mom and him the perfect memorial. He gave Bill the job of getting it done and to Ohio, no matter the cost. That was no small task for my brother and if he reads this, I publicly thank you for your labors for Dad. You have fulfilled one of God's great commandments to "Honor your mother and father." Dad was very specific to what he had engraved on this pure white piece of marble.

His humble nature is personified in this memorial slab of rock. His name, birthdate, and death all cover less than ten percent of the piece. Mom gets equal coverage, but their wedding date gets very special treatment with rings and banners. It is a great testament to his love and devotion to mom. The entire backside of this monument is devoted to their children, in order of birth, in line, and equal in font size, not only to each other's, but to his name and mom's as well! I know that he pressed both Bill and the stone cutter until the stone made the long trip from Colorado to Rushsylvania and he was overseer until it was set over his burial plot. At the time I found it somewhat silly of how happy and proud Dad was of this accomplishment, but now, I revere his diligence to be remembered not as a war hero or wealthy, prominent man of the community, but as a loving family man.

The story of this stone doesn't end here but I will return to it in order of events.

Dad put his finances in order. He and mom spent many hours with estate managers and lawyers to set up a trust for mom. He was very diligent in making sure mom would want for nothing.

As time moved on, Dad became more forgetful. He also seemed to become more passionate about certain truths he felt were being denied. That is hard to explain so I won't. I'll just say that he could get aggravated very easily but just as quickly, be happy again.

Along with what was going on in his mind, Dad began having other physical ailments. He developed lumps in his body which at the time seemed more like a nuisance than anything. He was still driving and going to the barn every day to "work". One cold morning, Brother

Jack and I stopped back at his shop to check on him. We found him working on a space heater. This is what heated the shop and for some reason he couldn't get it to work. It only took a minute for us to realize that instead of filling the tank with diesel fuel, Dad had filled the tank with gasoline. Romans 8:28 NKJV says: "And we know that all things work together for good to them that love God, to them who are called according to his purpose." I see this episode in our lives as a blessing. It was revealed to Jack and I that Dad was no longer safe doing what he had always done by himself. From here on out, he would need guidance so as not to hurt or kill himself or others. God was so very present with us that day. He kept that heater from exploding which probably would have killed Dad. He also showed my father the degree to which Dad's thought processes had deteriorated. Nothing needed to be said. Dad knew.

It has been seventeen years since these events and my memory is foggy with the exact order of how things transpired, but that's not as important as to how we as a family were led to Dad's leaving this world.

After a few months of seeing doctors for several symptoms, Dad's dentist suggested that one of the lumps on his jaw should be checked for cancer. There was a biopsy done and an oncologist called in. I find it amazing that my brothers and I were available to go to the hospital on the day his report was read. We all three were very busy at the time and Bill just happened to be here from Colorado so it was odd that we all would be with mom and Dad for just the latest of many doctor visits. I don't remember what they were doing with Dad at the time, but I do remember being in an examining room with Jack, Bill, mom and the doctor. I was oblivious to what this doctor might say. Jack and I had been goofing around like two kids up to this point. The doctor was very factual and to the point. He told us that Dad had a very aggressive form of cancer that was going to kill him in a matter of weeks.

It was like someone had punched me in the face.

As I tried to clear my mind and get a grip on what he had just said, I observed my family, who apparently felt the same blow. Bill (I believe) was holding mom. Maybe Jack too. I think I was the first to say anything. "You can't say that. How do you know he is only going to live a few weeks!" The doctor calmly stated, "Well I know this type of cancer and it progresses very rapidly. I've seen some patients fight it for a few months but it's rare". One of us asked "How do we tell Dad?" To which he replied "Let's don't say anything to upset him just yet. I want to run some more tests before I give him the final prognosis. I want to be sure". He told us that he would see Dad in two weeks when the final results were in. Those next two weeks were the most agonizing weeks of my life. Being with Dad, knowing the situation, and not saying anything was hard. How was he going to react when he found out? Would he be mad at us for not telling him? He seemed so innocent to have this verdict coming down on him.

Brother Bill had to go back to Colorado to run his business, but Jack and I went with mom and Dad for that next visit. I wanted to throw up. Dad was in his normal good mood when the doctor came in. Dad was sitting on the table and the doctor walked up to him, put his hands on Dad's arms, looked him straight in the eyes and said "Mr. Roberts, you have cancer and it's the Cadillac of cancers. You are only going to live for about six weeks". I almost fell down. This was worse than the first time I heard it. I watched for Dad to erupt in tears or wailing or something but what I saw was by far the greatest act of grace and bravery that I have ever witnessed. Dad said, "Well thank you for being so honest. I've been trying to get an answer from doctors for months and you're the first one to tell me the truth." I don't remember much of the rest of that visit; I was fighting so hard with my own thoughts and emotions. I do remember mom saying after the doctor walked out, "Oh Harry, wasn't he the nicest man." I remember thinking, "Nicest man!" He just told you that your husband is going to die.

I need to share a truth with you at this point. At this time in my life, I believed in God, but I wasn't living for him or depending on him. I could do alright on my own. What a horrible way to think.

This is the best time to go back to the war. As I mentioned in that chapter, Dad talked about certain events very casually, but near his death, they became terribly real to him.

Dad had received a book or two, I assume that had come from the army, which were the historical events and maps of what he had been through. He would read and reread parts of these books in his last days as if he was searching for an answer to something. If you asked him what he was reading about he would immediately engage you in what he was reading and tell you his place in the story. His memory seemed to become so much more vivid on this subject and the more he studied it the more emotional he became. He showed me the map of the town where he saw the two soldiers shot and relived that story, but now with all the detail that he had kept in his heart for all those years.

When the first soldier got killed, the whole platoon fell out and got to cover. After careful searching and finding nothing, they reformed and proceeded down the street. When later on, the man beside my Dad got shot, Dad not only saw the man drop dead, but he also saw the shooter straight down the alley from him. He saw the shooter head down the parallel street. When everyone else fell out, Dad ran down the street and beat the sniper to the next ally. When the shooter came through, Dad was waiting. Dad shot this man, and it grieved his heart to no end. As Dad sobbed, he asked why he had to make Dad shoot him! He also cried that this was such a young man!

Not many of us know what war is really like. Fewer still ever see up close the results of their actions. I know how much my father loved and cared for others. How hard a burden for him to bear all those years by himself. I'm reminded of the song "What a Friend We Have in Jesus". I remember as a child sitting in the pew as we sang those words.

What A Friend We Have In Jesus, by Joseph Scriven

What a friend we have in Jesus
All our sins and griefs to bear
What a privilege to carry
Everything to God in prayer
Oh, what peace we often forfeit
Oh, what needless pain we bear
All because we do not carry
Everything to God in prayer
Have we trials and temptations?
Is there trouble anywhere?
We should never be discouraged
Take it to the Lord in prayer
Can we find a friend so faithful
Who will all our sorrows share?
Jesus knows our every weakness
Take it to the Lord in prayer

I believe this song and the song "God is just a prayer away" and his faith helped Dad through.

God is Just a Prayer Away by Ed Bowsman

God is not so far away,
He can hear you when you pray.
Go to Him in all that you do,
He'll see you through.
God is just a prayer away,
Meet Him each hour night or day
His ear is never closed to your cares and woes
God is just a prayer away,
Meet Him each hour night or day
His love so divine joins His heart and mine
For God is just a prayer away.

Final Days

About a month before Harry died, he told Bill or Jack that he was concerned about his headstone. Because it is so white, you couldn't read the engraving. Because he never asked or complained about things like this, we knew something had to be done. Collectively we decided to see if we could get someone to paint in the engraving to make the letters stand out. My personal concern was that marble is very porous and colors may bleed into the stone. I contacted a professional sign painter (also a personal friend) and he assured us that he could do the job. Fortunately, he was able to do it within a short period of time. About two weeks before he died one of my brothers took Dad to the gravesite and he approved the work.

I was still having a hard time believing that he was that close to death. He was still engaging in conversations and was still getting around pretty good. However, I began to notice little changes. He started using a walker. Then we needed to help him go to the bathroom by helping him get up and down. We didn't have to clean him when he was done but I remember as we sat there that he usually had his eyes closed and would silently cry. I wondered at the time if he cried because it hurt or because of the humility he may have felt. Whatever it was didn't last long and he would be up and out without attention. I thank God that it was his family who went through this with him. Not just for his sake but ours as well. What grace comes from sharing in the suffering!

The day before he died, I stopped in to visit and to see if I could do anything to help. I will tell you at this point; all the family was eager to do the same. There was always someone there with mom and Dad during this time except for bedtime and even then, near the end, Amber, Bill's oldest daughter came and stayed. We all grew close around them. Dad was sitting in his recliner where he always sat, probably looking at one of his books or puzzle magazines. He told me," Those heifers' water is running down at the Old Brick, and someone needs to go shut it off." I said "Dad, there aren't any heifers down there anymore, there isn't even a pump to shut off." "I believe there is" he replied. I didn't want to argue with him, and something told me (now I know it was the Holy Spirit) to ask him if he wanted to take a ride down there and see. "I believe I would" he said and I could sense a feeling of purpose in him. I got him loaded into his pickup and we drove the short distance to where the Old Brick had stood. As I pulled into the drive my mind went back to the day that he ran the motorcycle gang out so many years before. Now, even the house itself was gone. He tore it down himself a few years earlier for safety reasons. His eyes looked sad as he slowly shook his head. "I'm just an old fool. I should have known they weren't here." he said as he stared into an empty lot. "That's okay. Since we're already out, how about we take a ride?" I asked. "Well, I think that's a good idea." he said with a lifted voice. So, we proceeded to drive around the neighborhood in which he had spent all seventy-eight years of his life. We didn't go by one place that he didn't make a comment on something that had happened in the past or was going on there now. It was delightful for both of us.

As we got close to home, I noticed a van parked in front of the house. It didn't take long to realize that it was the local hospice van. Hospice is a wonderful organization that helps families get through the final days of a loved one and I knew they would be coming sometime but why now? Dad and I had just had such a good time. He was able to get himself into the truck and seemed healthy enough to keep right on going. This wasn't good. I was sure that when he found out who it was, that he would at least have a meltdown. As we walked in the door, I noticed that furniture had been moved to accommodate this ugly hospital bed! He couldn't be happy about this. The hospice nurse, who was finishing making up the bed, said with a lilt in her voice "Hello Mr. Roberts. How would you like to try this new bed out?" Before I could even think of something to say to defray the situation for Harry, he says "Well sure!" That was at 5:30 in the evening. At about 1:00 a.m., mom called and said she didn't think Dad was going to make it through the night.

I have been witness to people dying in front of their loved ones since Dad died and I have recognized something very real and tangible in these situations that I may not have noticed if I wasn't present with my own family this night. The best way to explain it is seeing the hand or movement of God as he gently ministers to each one's heart as he brings back to himself those he has created. I feel compelled to go on one of my little preaches here for many reasons. The first one is 'This is my testimony. This is when I first really believed in a just and loving God and life after death. Someone once said that death will either draw you closer to God or farther away. I don't know who said it, but I believe it's a true statement. At least for me. 2nd Corinthians 7:10 NKJV

When Debbie and I walked in that night, there was an air about the room. It more than likely was just in my head, but everyone seemed to be acting differently. We were all more subdued than normal. All humbled by the event taking place in the same space that we had lived so hard and loud in all our lives. Each of us was careful to show our love and respect for the other. Each of us had time to tell this man that we loved him and goodbye. As I sat there and thought of all the good things this father of mine had done over the years, I was filled with humility and a repenting heart at what I could have done to honor him more. We all had our time to say what we were feeling both to Dad and one to another. Dad was not really conscious at this point. He was struggling with each breath he took. How could a man who took a ride with me just a few hours earlier have slipped to this horrible state so fast? My wife, Debbie, who is a paramedic and had worked with hospice for some time was very gracious to explain to us what was going on. Dad was given Morphine to help him with the pain, so he probably wasn't really hurting, but the sounds he made were hard to listen to. I realized that he wasn't ever going to get better in this world. As I listened to him struggle, I prayed the first real prayer I had prayed in a long time. "Dear God please take him now." Immediately his breathing stopped. I looked up in surprise and was looking right at sister Jill. She looked like a deer staring into headlights. We realized that he was gone. Debbie guided us through what had to be done. Soon the hospice nurse came and did her job. All the while I was filled with so much guilt. I had prayed for Dad to die, and he did. How cold is that just because I didn't want to suffer through his suffering. Later during the day, still feeling guilty about my prayer, I confessed to Jill what I had done. She grabbed my arm and said "Oh Joe. I did too!"

God was with us that night. He knew all our hearts. What a blessing Dad had passed. We couldn't have asked for more. From that time on, I know there is a God. I know where my earthly father now lives. Romans 8:18 NLT:

"Yet for what we suffer now is nothing compared to the glory he will reveal to us later."

During the next few days, we celebrated Harry Roberts's life. He had finished his race, I believe, as a good and faithful servant. I also believe he never tasted death but shed his old body like a coat and walked right into heaven. His funeral was a pleasant surprise to me as well. Of course, everyone is going to only say good things about the deceased but what I wasn't expecting were the people who came. I knew family, farmers, and church people would come, but oh my! Doctors and lawyers and many prominent business and civic leaders came. They all praised his righteous nature. Even the funeral home director graciously thanked the family and told me "Your father took care of everything way before his death."

The Bible teaches us that we are only here for a vapor of time. The wink of an eye. Seventeen years after Dad's death I am still amazed at how much he lived; how much he gave; how much he changed the lives around him for the better in that short period of time.

Printed in the United States
by Baker & Taylor Publisher Services